W9-BFY-121

Social Change and Family Processes

Brown University Studies in Population and Development

About the Book and Author

In this book, Majid Al-Haj analyzes the structure of family kinship groups, the role of women, and fertility among several Arab subcommunities in Israel. He combines historical materials, anthropological evidence, and several major surveys in tracing family and demographic patterns in a developing Arab community. This study is the first to compare Moslems, Christians, and Druze over time in the same community and to integrate issues of modernization and population for minorities. Particular attention is given to the analysis of "internal refugees" among Moslems, the separation of structural from cultural determinants of family patterns, and the distinction between behavior and norms associated with family lifestyles. This volume represents a fascinating case study of an Arab town in the transition to modernity under the conditions of changing layers of minority status in Israeli society. Moreover, the author addresses broader issues of modernization and demographic change characterizing the Middle East and other developing areas of the world where minority ethnic conflict and population processes are intertwined.

Majid Al-Haj teaches sociology and anthropology at Haifa University in Israel and was a postdoctoral fellow at the Population Studies and Training Center, Brown University.

**Brown University Studies
in Population and Development**

**Published in cooperation
with the Population Studies and Training Center
Brown University**

Editor
Calvin Goldscheider

Editorial Board

Sidney Goldstein
Philip Leis
Morris D. Morris
Alden Speare, Jr.

Social Change and Family Processes

Arab Communities in Shefar-A'm

Majid Al-Haj

Westview Press / Boulder and London

Brown University Studies in Population and Development

This Westview softcover edition is printed on acid-free paper and bound in softcovers that carry the highest rating of the National Association of State Textbook Administrators, in consultation with the Association of American Publishers and the Book Manufacturers' Institute.

All rights reserved. No part of this publication may be reproduced or transmitted in any form or by any means, electronic or mechanical, including photocopy, recording, or any information storage and retrieval system, without permission in writing from the publisher.

Copyright © 1987 by Westview Press, Inc.

Published in 1987 in the United States of America by Westview Press, Inc.; Frederick A. Praeger, Publisher; 5500 Central Avenue, Boulder, Colorado 80301

Library of Congress Cataloging-in-Publication Data
Al-Haj, Majid.
  Social change and family processes.
  (Brown University studies in population and
development; no. 4)
  Bibliography: p.
  1. Palestinian Arabs—Israel—Social conditions.
2. Palestinian Arabs—Israel—Family relationships.
3. Family—Israel.   4. Family life surveys—Israel.
5. Israel—Social conditions.   I. Title.   II. Series.
DS113.7.A63 1987   306.8′0899275694   86-28262
ISBN 0-8133-7325-5

Composition for this book was provided by the author.
This book was produced without formal editing by the publisher.

Printed and bound in the United States of America

The paper used in this publication meets the requirements of the American National Standard for Permanence of Paper for Printed Library Materials Z39.48-1984.

6   5   4   3   2   1

Contents

Tables

Figures and Maps

Figure

Map

Foreword

This volume in the continuing series of Brown University Studies in Population and Development is unique in its emphasis on family process and its focus on the Arab community in Israel. Although the family connections to demographic and sociological aspects of development have been noted in the literature, this research by Majid Al-Haj has significantly increased our understanding of the processes underlying these connections. He has done this by carrying out the analysis of the Arab community in Israel in new and creative ways. Several innovative features of his research include:

* A major focus of the analysis is on the community context, integrating micro-individual and macro-national levels. It is in the local community that the nuances of ethnic variation and change are most conspicuous and where group differences tend to manifest themselves most clearly.

* The methodological approach is interdisciplinary, dealing with the family from anthropological and sociological perspectives and incorporating demographic orientations to families and households. The approach moves beyond an oversimplified notion of family structure to identify the multiple layers at the kinship, extended, and nuclear family levels, and deals effectively with the complexities associated with variation and change in the status of women and fertility patterns.

* Particular attention is addressed to the dynamics of social change within the Arab community, in the context of the broader society. These changes among Arabs and between Arabs and Jews in Israel are critical for understanding the family patterns analyzed in this research. The multiple comparisons necessitated by this approach have been often neglected in social science studies based on surveys or field work in developing nations. Statistical and other historical records cover a period of three-quarters of a century from the early decades of the 20th century to the contemporary period.

* All too often the Arab community has been treated as a homogeneous community and at best only crude differences among religious groups are identified. Dr. Al-Haj has analyzed important distinctions among Moslem, Christian and Druze subcommunities within an urban town of the State of Israel and has examined important distinctions within them as well. The analysis of the "internal refugees" among Israeli Moslems is a particularly important feature of the analysis.

* The careful examination of social change in the family patterns of Arabs within the community has led to the separation of structural from the cultural determinants and has distinguished between behavior and norms associated with family lifestyles.

These contributions unfold in their theoretical complexities and are disentangled by methodological innovations that clarify family structural patterns, kin relations, the role and status of women, and the issues associated with fertility, contraception, and reproduction. No previous study of Arabs, in general, or Israeli Arabs, in particular, presents such a rich analysis of family variation and change in the context of sociological and demographic aspects of development.

This study is therefore more than a case study of an Arab town in Israel. Arabs in Israel share larger spheres of culture, religion, and nationality with millions of Arabs living in neighboring countries of the Middle East. Moreover, they share social and demographic features of high but declining fertility levels, an emphasis on traditional family values and women status, shifts from agriculture toward urban lifestyles and occupations, new forms of economic and political dependencies, and the continuing importance of ethnic and religious differentiation in modernizing societies. While illuminating the particulars of the community under investigation and the society of which it is a part, major issues of social and demographic change in the process of development are clarified.

The diverse theoretical themes covered in this monograph required the use of multi-level research strategies to obtain a wide range of evidence to test out complex hypotheses. Dr. Al-Haj uses an unusually wide range and diverse types of data sets, rare in the study of population and development issues. Included among these sources are the standard materials used by demographers (official data from census and vital statistics), by sociologists (sample surveys), by anthropologists (participant observation and qualitative field interviews, some with key informants), and by historians (archival materials, life histories, and personal diaries). The uniqueness of Dr. Al-Haj's research lies in the combination of all these diverse sources in a rich panoply of analysis and insight. His own participant observation in the community provided access to these diverse materials and facilitated their judicious use. More importantly, his detailed personal observations and involvement in the community provided the insight and sensitivity that moves his analysis beyond the routine.

I met Majid Al-Haj when he was completing his doctoral research in the Department of Sociology and Anthropology at the Hebrew University in Jerusalem. Recognizing the importance of demographic issues to his more social anthropological approach, he included questions of fertility and contraception in the context of his research on family lifestyles among Arabs in Israel. He saw the need to expand that part of his research and integrate a broader range of development issues within his analysis. He was responsive to the opportunity to spend a post doctoral year at the Population Studies and Training Center and the Department of Sociology at Brown University, to integrate sociological and demographic aspects of family and development issues.

As a post doctoral fellow at Brown, Dr. Al-Haj participated in seminars and organized formal presentations for the faculty and for the other post doctoral fellows in the program. He also made formal presentations to the broader graduate student audience and informally discussed with faculty issues of common research interest. In short, Majid Al-Haj became part of that special community that defines the intellectual life of sociologists and demographers at Brown.

He spent much of his time at Brown reorganizing, translating, and expanding his doctoral research for this monograph as well as for publication in various social science journals. Upon completion of his year, he returned to Haifa University in Israel to continue his research and teaching.

This volume adds to our series new methodological, theoretical, and substantial knowledge in the study of the linkages among family, population, and development processes. We are grateful to Mr. Edwin Jaffe and the Jaffe Foundation for supporting the research and the publication of these important materials. Carol Walker and Pat Savard were very helpful in bringing the manuscript into shape for publication. And our gratitude to Majid Al-Haj for teaching us through this research about relationships between population and development in an important area of the developing world.

Calvin Goldscheider
Brown University

Preface

Several studies have noted the importance of research on family patterns for the understanding of population and development in developing societies. This is because family is the basic unit of demographic and social behavior. The analysis of the relationship between family and social change is complex. At the family level, it necessitates distinguishing between the different familial units, from the broader unit (kinship group) to the nuclear unit. The analysis should encompass the nature of the interaction within each unit and among these units as well. At the broader level, it necessitates the understanding of the economic, political and demographic changes in the community and the wider society, on the one hand, and the linkages between them and the family, on the other. Our task becomes even more complicated when we have to trace the changes in this relationship over time, since we need a close follow-up of the changes occurring in all the variables at work. Community-level studies may be ideal for the analysis of family processes and development. They provide an in-depth documentation and wide understanding for the dynamics of the interaction between the individual, familial group, communal and societal levels.

In our study an attempt is made, for the first time, to employ an interdisciplinary approach, combining anthropological, sociological and demographic methods in order to trace family lifestyles in a developing Arab urban community in Israel (Shefar-A'm). We focus on three familial units: the kinship structure *(hamula)*, the extended family and the nuclear family. These units are examined within the context of the broader economic, political and socio-demographic process. Family patterns are investigated currently and over time using diachronic and synchronic analysis. We trace family lifestyles from the last years of the Ottoman period, through the Mandatory period (1918-1948), to the period following the establishment of the State of Israel. The investigation encompasses all the representative groups among Arabs in Israel: Moslems, Christians, Druze and other migratory groups. The dynamics of the interaction within and among these groups are examined in order to analyze the effect of the group status structure on family patterns.

Our analysis has shown that micro familial processes and macro sociological changes are mutually affected by each other. The relationship between them is changeable. It may change over time in response to changes in the broader economic and socio-cultural situation. The analysis suggests that modernization in family patterns occurs through complex processes of diversification, rather than through uniform overall processes. We have shown that diversification in the social structure and the family patterns is not restricted to the modern industrial period, but may emerge as well in agrarian societies, usually defined as traditional. Our study shows that processes of modernization are determined more by structural than cultural or psychological factors.

The book includes seven major chapters. Chapter 1 presents the main research interests including the examination of family patterns and their relationships with broader population and development factors. We discuss the research strategy, theoretical framework, major questions and the research methods. Chapter 2 deals with the economic, demographic and group status structure of the community under research. We examine the social history of the community, the major changes occurring after the establishment of Israel, and the changes over time in the internal and the external modes of dependence. The group status structure is analyzed in the framework of minority-majority model including the effect of both the communal and the societal factors.

Chapters 3-6 present our analysis of the family patterns. Chapter 3 deals with the status of the kinship structure, the definition of the kinship group, its characteristics and functioning. We discuss the political, the social and the economic roles of the *hamula* in terms of actual behavior as well as at the normative levels. Chapter 4 analyzes the extended family structure, its changing characteristics and roles. The different types of extended family are analyzed along with the changing modes of production, social class structure and other broader economic and demographic processes. Two central issues are selected to investigate the nuclear family: Women status and fertility and family planning. Chapter 5 deals with women status at home and the community. We discuss the relationship between actual status of women and the normative ideological system. The resource theory and the modernization approach are applied to analyze the determinants of women status. Chapter 6 deals with patterns of fertility among the different groups in the community under research. Group differentials in fertility and family planning are analyzed by juxtaposition of four theoretical hypotheses: the family planning hypothesis, the characteristics hypothesis, the minority status hypothesis and the Westernization hypothesis. The concluding chapter (Chapter 7) examines the implications of our analysis for the study of family life styles and the relationship between social change and family processes. We discuss the significance of the experience derived from our field study, the extent of the effectiveness of the theoretical framework for the analysis of family and some recommendations for future family studies.

Of the many friends and colleagues who encouraged me in several ways in writing this book I wish to thank first and foremost Professor Calvin Goldscheider of the Sociology Department at Brown University. He encouraged me to add to my socio-anthropological background the demographic tools for analysis. This book could not have been completed without his extensive guidance and detailed comments. Throughout my stay at Brown he showed endless patience in responding to my queries concerning the complexity of the subject of family and social change. I am also very grateful to Professor Henry Rosenfeld of the University of Haifa and Professor Erik Cohen of the Hebrew University in Jerusalem, who through their guidance in the doctoral thesis encouraged me to sharpen my concepts concerning the research on Arabs in Israel and putting the analysis of the Arab family in a universal context. Special thanks are also due to Professor Sidney Goldstein, the director of the Population Studies and Training Center at Brown University, for his helpful comments on Chapters 3 and 6. Thanks to the Hewlett Foundation and the Jaffe Foundation for their financial support of my post-doctoral fellowship at Brown. I am particularly indebted to the encouragement of Mr. Edwin Jaffe, the Chairman of the Jaffe Foundation. Carol Walker typed the materials for this book expertly and Kathy Eckstrand helped in editing the manuscript. My thanks to Professor Sami Mari, Sammy Smooha, Avner Yaniv and Arnon Soffer of the Haifa University for their encouragement through my academic work. My gratitude to my wife, who helped me to overcome many difficulties in coping with both my academic work and family commitments.

Majid Al-Haj
Haifa University
Israel

مقدمـــة

تشغل دراسة مبنى العائلة والتبدل الاجتماعي حيزا هاما من الدراسات التي تجري في المجتمعات النامية والتي تسمى بالعالم الثالث . فالعائلة هي وحدة اجتماعية مركزية يتخذ من خلالها الكثير من القرارات الهامة التي تنعكس بالتالي على الفرد والمجتمع وتلعب دورا اساسيا في مسار التطور والتبدل . لكن العائلة بدورها تتأثر بالتغيرات الاقتصادية ، السياسية والاجتماعية التي تحدث نتيجة لعوامل خارجية مختلفة ، من هنا فدراسة العلاقة بين العائلة والمجتمع تحتم النظر الى هــذه العلاقة على انهـا ديناميكية ، متبادلة وقابلة للتبدل والتغير .

لقد تركزت الدراسات التي اجريت حول العائلة العربية في اسرائيل وفي المجتمعات العربية الشرق اوسطية حول وحدتين اساسيتين : الحمولـة والعائلة الموسعة وتطرق عدد قليل منها نسبيا الى العائلة النواة مع انها تعتبر الوحدة العائلية المركزية اليوم. بالاضافة لذلك فقليلة هي الدراسات التي تطرقت للوحدات العائلية الثلاث في آن واحد لبحث ديناميكية العلاقة داخل هذه الوحدات من جهة وبينها وبين المجتمع المحلي والمجتمع العــام من جهة اخرى . لقد تمحورت الدراسات التي تطرقت الى العائلة العربية في اسرائيل حول المجتمعات القروية والبدوية وتطرق القليل منها فقط الى مجتمع المدينة . لم تذكر هذه الدراسات الا النزر اليسير عن المقارنة بين اساليب الحياة العائلية لدى المجموعات المختلفة داخل المجتمع العربـي نفسه وبعض هذه المجموعات لم ينل أي اهتمام ، فاللاجئون الداخليــون مثلا ، الذين انتقلوا الى قرى ومدن مختلفة داخل اسرائيل بعد أن هدمت قراهم نتيجة لحرب ١٩٤٨ ، لم يحظوا حتى بالقليل من الاهتمام بالرغـم من اشارة التقديرات الاخيرة الى ان واحد من كل اربعة عرب في اسرائيل هو لاجىء أو ابن لعائلة لاجئين .

ان هذا الكتاب الذي بين ايديكم هو ثمرة جهد سنوات مـن الدراسة والتمحيص حول اساليب الحياة العائلية وعلاقتها بالتبدلات الاجتماعيـة السياسية والاقتصادية . لقد اختيرت مدينة شفاعمرو كمكان لاجراء هذه الدراسة الميدانية للبحث المعروض في الكتاب نتيجة لاعتبارات موضوعية متعددة ، فمن حيث الاهمية التاريخية ، حظيت شفاعمرو بمركز تاريخـي هام على مر العصور . ففي سنة ١٩١٠ استفادت شفاعمرو من القانون العثماني الذي صدر سنة ١٩٠٨ ونص على أن كل بلدة تستعمل كمركـز مديرية يجب أن تدار عن طريق مجلس بلدي منتخب . وهكذا كانـت

شفاعمرو من أولى البلديات في منطقة شمال البلاد . لقد كان لاهمية شفاعمرو الادارية والاقتصادية ووقوعها على مفترق طرق بين المـدن الرئيسية حيفا ، عكا والناصرة دورا كبيرا في جذب الهجرة اليها مـن مناطق مختلفة . نتيجة لذلك فقد سكنها ابناء جميع الديانات علـى مـر العصور ، واليوم تعتبر شفاعمرو أحد الاماكن النادرة التي يوجد بهـا عينات ممثلة لجميع العرب في اسرائيل على اختلاف طوائفهم وفئاتهـم : مسلمون ، مسيحيون ودروز وعشائر بدوية، مهاجرون من القرى المجاورة ولاجئون نتيجة للحرب سنة ١٩٤٨ . بالرغم من أن الهجرة الداخلية الى القرى والمدن العربية في اسرائيل كانت قليلة جدا نسبيا بعد قيام الدولة فقد استمر تيار الهجرة الى شفاعمرو دون انقطاع نتيجة لدمجها بين الطابع القروي وطابع المدينة ، ونتيجة لقربها من المناطق اليهودية الصناعيـة وسهولة المواصلات اليهـا ، مما زاد من تعدديـة سكانها والانكشاف لانماط مختلفة من العادات ، التقاليد واساليب الحياة العائلية

لقد تطرق البحث الـى التبدلات والتطورات الرئيسية التي حدثت في الوحدات العائلية الثلاث في المجتمع العربي (الحمولة ، العائلة الموسعـة والعائلة النواة) . تغطي الدراسة فترة طويلة من الزمن تمتد منذ نهايـة الحكم العثماني في اوائل هذا القرن مارة بفترة الانتداب (١٩١٨ – ١٩٤٨) وبعد قيام دولة اسرائيل . نتيجة لشمولية الدراسة وجمعها بين جوانـب مختلفة من اساليب الحياة العائلية ، المجتمع المحلي والمجتمع الخارجي راينا اتباع منهجا دراسيا يجمـع في آن واحـد عددا مـن المناهـج السوسيولوجية ، الانثروبولوجية والديموغرافية المتبعة ، فقد تم جمـع وتحليل آلاف الوثائق التي تتعلق بالتاريخ الاجتماعي للبلدة ، مسألـة الاراضي ، المبنى الاقتصادي والسياسي ، العلاقات بين المجموعـات المختلفة ، العلاقات داخل العائلة وبين العائلة والمجتمع الاوسع . جمعت هذه الوثائق من البلدية ومكاتب رسمية أخرى ، المحكمة الشرعية ، القرى المجاورة ووثائق خاصة من السكان مـن مختلف العائلات والطوائـف في البلدة . بالاضافة لذلك فقد أجري مسح شامل لجميع العائلات التي لها أولاد في المراحل التعليمية المختلفة من سن البستان وحتى التعليم الثانوي تم التعرف من خلاله على الميزات الرئيسية للعائلات في شفاعمرو مثـل ثقافة الوالدين ، المهنة ، القرابة العائلية قبل الزواج ، السكن ومتغيرات هامة أخرى . وقد تم اختيار عينة ممثلة من الاسر في شفاعمرو وأجريت ٢٤٠ مقابلة مع الزوجين حول الجوانب المختلفة للحياة العائلية ، العلاقات داخل العائلة بين الزوج والزوجة ، الوالدين والابناء ، الاجيال المختلفة وبين العائلة النواة والوحدات العائلية والاجتماعية الاوسع . هذا بالاضافة

الى عدد من المعطيات الشاملة التي استقت من تقارير اقسام البلدية ومحطة تنظيم الاسرة في البلدة . اجري عدد كبير من المقابلات العميقة مع شخصيات بمراكز قيادية ومهنية مختلفة نخص منها بالذكر : السيد ابراهيم نمر حسين رئيس البلدية ، المرحوم جبور جبور رئيس البلدية السابق السيد خليل مشيعل سكرتير مجلس العمال ، الدكتور محمود عباسي مساعد وزير المعارف والثقافة سابقا ، الدكتور موفق دياب ، الدكتور جمال حسون ، السيد روحي كركبي مدير البنك العربي ، السيد جورج فرح مدير بنك العمال ، السيد حسن ذياب مدير مكتب العمل والسيد أحمد حمدي سكرتير فرع شفاعمرو للحزب الشيوعي .

يحوي الكتاب سبعة فصول رئيسية . يعرض الفصل الاول نقاط البحث الرئيسية ، استراتيجية ومنهج الدراسة ، مدخل نظري واهم الاسئلة المطروحة ، يبحث الفصل الثاني في المبنى الاقتصادي والسكاني لشفاعمرو والمبنى السياسي للمجموعات المختلفة . يتطرق هذا الفصل الى المبنى الاجتماعي للبلدة والتغيرات الرئيسية التي حصلت بعد قيام الدولة . الفصول ٣ — ٦ تستعرض أساليب الحياة العائلية وديناميكية العلاقة داخل العائلة وخارجها . يتركز الفصل الثالث حول مبنى الحمولة واختلاف وظائفها الاجتماعية ، السياسية والاقتصادية على مر الفترات . في الفصل الرابع نستعرض العائلة الموسعة والتبدلات في ميزاتها ووظائفها نتيجة للتغيرات في مبنى الانتاج والتحولات الاخرى في المجتمع المحلي والخارجي . لقد اخترنا مسألتين رئيسيتين لبحث موضوع العائلة النواة : مركز المراة وتنظيم الاسرة ، يتطرق الفصل الخامس لمركز المراة في البيت والمجتمع ، الايديولوجية الثقافية التى تؤثر على مركز المراة ووظائفها وانعكاسات الجوانب المختلفة لمسيرة التمدن التي يمر بها المجتمع العربي في اسرائيل، يحوي الفصل السادس استعراضا وتحليلا للانماط المختلفة لتنظيم الاسرة لدى المجموعات المختلفة في البلدة حيث تفسر هذه الفروقات على خلفية عدد من النظريات المعروفة . نستعرض في التلخيص (الفصل السابع) الابعاد المختلفة للدراسة المعروضة بالنسبة لقضية العلاقة بين التبدل الاجتماعي والعائلة في المجتمعات النامية ، مدى فعالية النظريات المختلفة في تفسير هذه العلاقة والرؤيا المستمدة من هذا البحث لدراسات مستقبلية حول الموضوع .

انتهز هذه المقدمة ، التي كتبت خصيصا باللغة العربية ، لاعبر عن اعتزازي الكبير بالتشجيع الذي لمسته من اخواني ابناء شفاعمرو الكرام خلال مراحل دراستي المختلفة . لقد كان للتعاون الذي لقيته منهم الاثر الاكبر في اغناء هذه الدراسة بالمعلومات والحقائق الشاملة والتي نعرض

الكثير منها لأول مرة . لقد لمست هذا التعاون في المقابلات مع العائلات المحادثات المستفيضة ، الاتصالات مع المؤسسات العامة وفي البحث عن الوثائق الرسمية والشخصية . أتقدم بشكري الجزيل الى الأخ ابراهيم نمر حسين ، أبو حاتم ، رئيس بلدية شفاعمرو ، لقد أعطتني فرصة العمل معه كمدير لقسم المعارف في البلدية لمدة خمس سنوات وأحاديثنا المتواصلة حول مواضيع مختلفة فرصة ثمينة لفهم الجوانب المختلفة في المجتمع . أشكر جميع الذين زودوني بكل ما لديهم من وثائق ، كان الكثير منها شخصيا جدا وأخص منهم بالذكر السيد عزات توفيق داهود ، أبو توفيق ، من قرية عبلين الذي زودنا بوثائق هامة حول قضية الأرض وعلاقات شفاعمرو بالقرى المجاورة ، السيد رشيد بولس ، أبو سامي ، الذي زودنا بجميع دفاتر المذكرات النادرة للمرحومين والده وجده ، والتي تغطي تقريبا بشكل يومي فترة تمتد على مدى قرن من الزمن . أشكر عائلة الشيخ محمد أبو عبيد على تزويدنا بجمع الوثائق والمذكرات الشخصية والعامة التي تتعلق بالطائفة الدرزية وعلاقتها خارج شفاعمرو الشيخ سعد نكد الذي زودنا بالسجلات الهامة عن توزيع الأراضي بشفاعمرو ، السيد محمد خازم والسيد يوسف مباريكي على الوثائق الشخصية والمذكرات ، أشكر رجال الدين للطوائف الثلاث الذين زودونا بسجلات الزواج وقدموا ملاحظاتهم الهامة لتحليل هذه السجلات ، السيد علي أحمد خطيب مأذون الطائفة الاسلامية ، الأب كرولس حبيب خوري الطائفة الكاثوليكية والمرحوم الشيخ سلمان أبو عبيد امام الطائفة الدرزية سابقا . كما وأشكر جميع مدراء المدارس الابتدائية والثانوية لتعاونهم البناء وجميع الذين أجريت معهم المقابلات والأحاديث القيمة .

لقد أعددت هذا الكتاب باللغة الانجليزية خلال تواجدي في جامعة براون بالولايات المتحدة لفترة استكمال ما بعد الدكتوراة . أتقدم بشكري الجزيل لجميع المحاضرين بكلية علم الاجتماع في الجامعة ، وأخص منهم بالذكر البرفسور غولدشايدر والبرفسور غولدستين والسيد جافي على تشجيعهم لاخراج هذا الكتاب الى النور ، كما وأشكر البرفسور هنري روزنفلد المحاضر بجامعة حيفا والبرفسور آريك كوهين المحاضر بالجامعة العبرية الذين تعلمت من خبرتهما الشيء الكثير خلال ارشادهما لي لاعداد اجازة الدكتوراة في الجامعة العبرية .

وأخيرا وليس آخرا أتقدم بشكري الحار الى والدتي التي تعلمت منها الدروس الأولى في المثابرة والجد ، وزوجتي التي وقفت بجانبي ومنحتني التشجيع الذي له فضل كبير في ما وصلت اليه ....

ماجد الحاج

1

Theoretical Contexts for Studying Israeli Arabs

The study of family structure, attitudes, and decision making is crucial for understanding population and socioeconomic development processes (Ford and DeJong, 1970). As the basic unit in demographic and social behavior, the family is an integral part of development and demographic changes. On the one hand, the family plays an important role in creating and affecting these changes; on the other, it is strongly affected by them (Wrigley, 1960; Wrong, 1977). Community-level studies of family patterns have been emphasized as one of the important research targets for future social research. The significance of such studies lies in their capacity to provide in-depth documentation of family structure, family characteristics, interrelationships among family members, family functioning, and the relationship between the family and the broader demographic, economic, and political processes (see Miro and Potter, 1980; Poplin, 1972).

The investigation of family patterns necessitates making a distinction among several family units; in particular, the kinship group, the extended family, and the nuclear family. The characteristics of each unit and the nature of the relationship among the several units may have a different impact on population and socioeconomic factors. For example, the status of the kinship group and the extended family has been inversely related to the status of the nuclear family. If the extended family has a high status, decision making within the nuclear family is restricted, the roles of women are constrained, and young spouses are less able to determine their family affairs. These include central aspects of family and social life--reproduction consumption, and other family decisions. In the extended family structure, matchmaking is determined mainly by the family, not by the individual. Family size is not determined solely by the spouses, but rather is influenced by other family members. The efforts and production of the family members, including children, are directed to serve the extended family, where the role of individuals is eliminated (see Caldwell, 1977; Al-Nouri, 1980; Galal el-Din, 1977). Therefore, it has been repeatedly argued that the demographic transition to controlled fertility and small family size is connected with the nucleation of the family, the reinforcement of women's status, and the change in the direction and magnitude of intergenerational wealth flows from parents to children (Caldwell, 1977:81).

Changes in family units are not isolated from broader economic, political and demographic changes. Family structure have always been linked to modes of production (Nimkoff and Middleton, 1960). Ethnic and religious conflicts, territorial differences in economic opportunity, and the uprooting of peoples by war have been noted as major determinants of migration (Wrong, 1977). Economic dependency and the lack of access to the opportunity structure have been noted as major barriers for modernizing these groups and, in turn, for changing their family patterns (Goldscheider, 1981). The relationships between micro familial changes and macro sociological processes are dynamic; they may change over time in response to changes in the broader economic and socio-cultural situation (see Bilsborrow, 1981).

These theoretical considerations have implications for the ways in which family patterns need to be studied and the development of appropriate and effective research strategies. The several familial units have to be analyzed simultaneously in an integrated way. Only in this way can there by an in-depth understanding of the nature of the interaction between the nuclear family and the other extended familial units and the examination of the effects of changes in one familial unit on the other. A linkage should be made between family patterns and broader economic, demographic, and political changes. In this sense, we have to take into consideration community-level factors, including economic and political structure, services, group status structure, and related variables. Individual, familial, group, communal, and societal levels have to be delineated and analyzed in the framework of a dynamic model of interaction. Family patterns have to be analyzed currently and over time in order to trace changes in family life and to understand the nature of the relationships among the family units and the broader processes.

2

The Arab society in Israel is an ideal place for the application of the above research strategy and the investigation of the relationship between family patterns and population and socioeconomic development. Despite the particular political position of Arabs in Israel, they share many common features with developing Middle Eastern societies: culture, nationality, language, and religion. Most importantly, they have similar levels of high fertility and a pattern of delayed demographic transition to small family size. In addition, they have the same religious group differences in terms of fertility, where Moslems have the highest fertility rates, followed by Druze and then Christians (see Yaukey; 1961; Chamie, 1977; Friedlander and Goldscheider, 1979, 1984).

Until the last years (1940s) of the Mandatory Period, when the British controlled Palestine, Arabs were an agrarian society in which the extended family structure was central, with the clear dominance of men over women (Rosenfeld, 1964, 1968). The political, economic, and demographic changes which occurred after the establishment of the state of Israel have had major repercussions on Arabs in Israel. Arabs went from a majority to a minority population constituting only about 12 percent of the total population (Ben-Amram, 1965). The Arab-Israel war in 1948 resulted in the destruction of several hundred Arab villages. The vast majority of their residents became external refugees in neighboring Arab countries or internal refugees within Israel (Peretz, 1958).

Drastic economic changes have also taken place. They have resulted in the occupational transformation from agricultural work within Arab localities to wage labor in the Jewish sector. A substitute local economic base has not been created and Arabs have become more and more dependent economically on the Jewish dominant sector (Rosenfeld, 1964; Smooha, 1980). The intense contact with the Jewish population, who represent for Israeli Arabs the agents of westernization, has exposed Arabs to a new sociocultural experience which has great potential influence on many aspects of their lifestyle (Avitsour, 1978).

Social research on Middle Eastern societies as well as on Arabs in Israel has lacked some of the major components of the research strategy outlined above. Most studies focusing on family and social change have been general and descriptive, rather than analytic (Rosenfeld, 1972). In this sense, fewer efforts have been made to analyze family patterns in the framework of a dynamic approach which takes into consideration the interactions among the family units and between them and the broader social units. Therefore, the linkage between the family structure and the broader demographic, economic, and social contexts has, for the most part, been eliminated (Allman, 1976). Middle Eastern societies have been described as traditional, changeless, and resistant to modernization, where Islamic culture constitutes the major barrier for change (see Rosenfeld, 1972; Caldwell, 1977; Patai, 1983). The past, the pre-modern period, has an often been viewed as an "unchanging traditional society". Much less effort has been made to trace the social history of the community as an integral part of understanding the present situation (Allman, 1978). Thus, change is inferred "when a situation or behavior is observed which differs from the described in the normative literature" (Van Dusen, 1976:6).

Some scholars have ignored the diversity in family lifestyles in the Middle East by treating the "Arab family" or the "Islamic family" as a whole (see Al-Faruqi, 1978). Berger (1962:118) noted, "Yet one can profitably discuss the Moslem family in general, because it displays certain patterns. This is a result of the strength of tradition in the Arab world, the confinement thus far of profound social change to the wealthier and more educated classes in the cities, and the pervading influence of Islam and its prescription for family life."

Studies conducted among Arabs in Israel have concentrated on two main familial units: the kinship structure and the extended family. But few studies have investigated the nuclear family and fewer have analyzed all three familial units in an integrated way. The vast majority of these studies have concentrated on rural communities or Bedouin tribes and few have studied urban communities within Israel. Moreover, some important groups among Arabs have seldom been analyzed. While Moslem and Druze family patterns have been researched, few studies relating to Christians and almost none to Arab internal refugees has been conducted.[1] Attempts to analyze these several groups in one comparative research are rarer still. (For a comprehensive review of the social research on Arabs in Israel, see Smooha and Cibulski, 1978; Smooha, 1984).

----

[1] Internal refugees were displaced from their communities as a result of the 1948 war and moved to other communities inside Israel. At present, they constitute one-fourth of the Arabs in Israel (Al-Haj, 1985). This group will be discussed in detail subsequently.

Our study does not attempt to eliminate all the deficiencies noted above. Nevertheless, an attempt is made for the first time to employ a combination of different comprehensive research methods in order to trace the family lifestyles in an Arab urban community in Israel (Shefar-A'm) through simultaneous analysis of the changes over time. We focus on the three main familial units within the context of the broader economic, political and socio-demographic processes. The study covers the time from the last years of the Ottoman period through the Mandatory period (1915-1947) to the post-1948 period following the establishment of the State of Israel. Family patterns are investigated currently and over time using a diachronic and synchronic analysis. The investigation encompasses all the representative groups among Arabs in Israel: Moslems, Christians, and Druze; and various migratory groups: internal refugees, Druze El-Jabal (who settled in the town during the late 1950s), and Bedouin (who moved to a stable settlement during the early 1960s).

Our analysis includes the three main familial units: the kinship structure, the extended family, and the nuclear family. More specifically, we investigate the status of the kinship structure, the key attributes and roles of the extended family, the status of women, and the patterns of fertility. Throughout our analysis, a clear distinction is made between the behavioral level (actual, behavior defined in terms "of which action in fact takes place") and the normative level (ideal, defined in terms "of which some specific set of actors think action should take place") (see Levy, 1965:7). In this sense, the concept of "family lifestyles" is both behavioral and normative. Family lifestyle refers to the salient structural attributes of the main familial units; the manner in which members of a given family try to take full advantage of their social, political, and cultural potential; the interaction among family members and between the family and its milieu at both the communal and the broader societal levels. The normative level includes the prevailing ideology in the community towards these aspects of family life and the family members perception of styles of family life--their own as well as other people's.

Theoretical Framework

The main purpose of using a theoretical framework in our analysis is to facilitate our understanding of family lifestyles among the several groups in Shefar-A'm and the nature of the relationship between family structure and the several analytical

5

levels: the individual, the group, the community, and the societal. We do not test a specific theory or a specific set of hypotheses. Therefore, in each of the main familial units, the prevailing theoretical approaches for the specific subject will be employed. In addition, we shall examine the modernization approach throughout our analysis. This approach is one of the most prevailing themes of social science (Goldscheider, 1981) and is central to the understanding of developing societies as well as Middle Eastern societies (see Schnaiberg, 1970; Caldwell, 1977; Rosenfeld, 1972; Goldscheider, 1982). Its advantage lies in the linkage it makes between family change and the wider evolution process (Goode, 1963). In the following discussion, we summarize the main components of the modernization approach and their repercussions on family life and on social research in the Middle East as well as on Arabs in Israel. We also outline briefly a counter theoretical framework --dependency theory.

The most salient of the several analytical units distinguished in the modernization approach are the international, societal, and individual units (see Nettle and Roberston, 1968; Lerner, 1964; Schnaiberg, 1970; Inkeles and Smith, 1974). But few studies have concentrated on the communal level (Goldscheider, 1981). The modernization approach in general posits that the process of change and modernization which has already taken place in the Western societies will sooner or later spread to the developing societies (Tippes, 1973; Inkeles and Smith, 1974). In this sense, modernization is the result of the acculturation of non-Western people to Western culture (Kanaana, 1975a). Therefore, "modern means being Western without the onus of dependence on the West" (Shils, 1965: 10). The Western component has been strongly emphasized so that some scholars have concentrated on the specific effect of westernization rather than on modernization as a whole (see Goode, 1963). Caldwell, for example, in his analysis of demographic transitions has placed particular emphasis on westernization as a subset of modernization. He suggested that the export of the European social and economic systems was central to the understanding of the fertility transition (Caldwell, 1977: 107).

At the societal level, modernization is linked to urbanization, the spread of education and literacy, and "presumably the development of an industrial urban base from which to support many of the educational and economic changes undergone by individual actors in the society" (Schnaiberg, 1970:419). At the individual level, a modern man may be summed as follows: he is informed, participant, and active; he has a marked sense of personal efficacy; he is highly independent and autonomous in his relations to traditional sources; he is ready for new experiences and innovation; and he places higher value on formal education and schooling (Inkeles and Smith, 1974:290).

The modernization approach presumes that modern attitudes and modern behavior are synonymous (Inkeles and Smith, 1974). Therefore, psychological modernity, which consists of modern attitudes, norms, and perceptions, is expected to lead to modern behavior and in turn to the modernity of the society as a whole. "Modernization consists of a variety of changes describable as changes in the content of mind. These changes constitute the cause rather than the product of change" (Spengler, 1974:153). The "take off" to modernity is conditioned by having a mobile personality (empathy) which implies a capacity for identification with the new aspects of one's environment (Lerner, 1964:49).

Some elementary postulates in the modernization approach have emerged. Modernization is an all encompassing process. The "breakthrough" of modernization can be achieved only by the "breakdown" of the antecedent traditional structure (Evers, 1975). The replacement of old traditions by new patterns of attitudes and behavior is the inevitable outcome of modernization. Therefore, modernization is viewed as the antithesis of traditionalism (Gusfield, 1967). This point has been strongly emphasized by students of modernization so that modern has been defined as "anything which has more or less recently replaced something which in the past was an accepted way of doing things" (Inkeles and Smith, 1974:15). This leads to the conclusion that traditional and modern approaches are always in conflict (Gusfield, 1967).

The modernization approach assumes unity in modernism and the modernizing process (Schnaiberg, 1970). A "modern man" is a cross-national phenomenon. The set of attitudes, values, and behaviors which constitutes the syndrome of modernity are transcultural. "What defines a man as modern in one country also defines him as such in other countries . . . . This led to the conclusion that there is not only a potential, but at least in one sense, an actual psychic unity in mankind" (Inkeles and Smith, 1974:118). In addition, the components of modernization are assumed to be interrelated. A person who has one modern characteristic would have other modern characteristics (Ibid; Schnaiberg, 1970).

Modern society has been viewed as a society with a high level of differentiation (Eisenstadt, 1975). Traditional society, in contrast, has been viewed as a homogeneous social structure (Gusfield, 1967). Modern societies are always oriented towards change which involves the search "for the conditions of such continued, sustained growth" (Eisenstadt, 1975:5). Therefore, the modernization process is continuous. At the individual level a cessation in modernity or a reversal towards more traditionalism is not expected (Inkeles and Smith, 1974). This leads to the conclusion that traditionalism and modernity are mutually exclusive systems (Palmore, Klein and Marzuki, 1970; Gusfield, 1967).

The spread of modernization occurs through mass media, mass education, and contact with agents of westernization (Caldwell, 1977). The effect of these agents, who are mostly Western people, colonial administrators, and missionaries (Kanaana, 1975a), is transferred to the traditional society through a specific small group of locals who may be called "innovators" (Goode, 1963; Caldwell, 1977). This group is the most westernized, the so-called "elite" who are "deemed to be the main exponents of a dynamism in pursuit of change. It is they on whom all hopes and expectations are set for introducing change in various fields" (Wertheim, 1975:97). In this sense, modernization is viewed as a positive phenomenon. It implies "the infusion of a rational and positive spirit" (Lerner, 1964:45). Western societies are presented more and more as successful models to be followed (Gusfield, 1967).

The focus of the modernization approach on cultural values and psychological attitudes as the main components of the development process and the assumption that developing societies will follow, sooner or later, the same modernization process experienced by developed Western societies has been severely criticized by students of the dependency theory. By focusing on individuals, modernization theory does not permit the consideration of the actual and the potential effects of the broader structural variables and the differential access to the opportunity structure (Valenzuela and Valenzuela, 1984). In addition, it is inappropriate to think that individual nations or groups in developing societies will somehow repeat the historical modernization of Western nations. Since "features of currently industrialized nations are products of unique historical processes which already belong to the mankind's past, the concrete features of advanced societies of today cannot be reproduced exactly in the future, nor is this the goal of most Third World nations" (Portes, 1976:74).

In contrast to modernization theory, the dependency perspective posits that differences in development levels between individuals, groups, and nations are the outcome of differences in

8

the access to the opportunity structure (Dos Santos, 1984; Portes, 1976). Therefore, what varies between traditional and modern societies "is not the degree of rationality, but the structural foundation of the incentive system which, in turn, produces different forms of behavior" (Valenzuela and Valenzuela, 1984:108). This approach emphasize issues of differential power and control of resources and, in turn, inequalities between groups and subgroups in order to understand the complexity of the modernization process (Goldscheider, 1981). Inequality may be imposed from the outside as a result of national dependencies or emerge within the same society as the result of internal colonialism (Goldscheider, 1981; Hechter, 1975; Smooha, 1978). However, in both cases, a powerful center with control over the several resources and a dependent periphery emerges. The periphery has a refiex type of development conditioned by the expansion of the center (Valenzuela and Valenzuela, 1984). This expansion can have either a positive or a negative effect on the immediate development of the periphery (Dos Santos, 1984). In this sense, the modernization of the periphery may be restricted because of the structural constraints imposed by the center (Portes, 1976).

Unlike the modernization approach, the dependency perspective posits that contact between developed, modernized groups and a less developed group or groups does not insure the modernization of the latter. Uneven modernization levels are expected to be observed as long as these groups have differential access to the opportunity structure (Smooha, 1978). The trend over time may not be towards a convergence in the development levels of the several groups, but rather the gap may be widened as the result of reinforcing dependency and inequalities (see Goldscheider, 1981; Seligson, 1984).

The postulates of the modernization approach are reflected in its hypotheses concerning family patterns. One of the basic assumptions of this approach has been that little variation exists in the family and the kinship structure in developing societies during the pre-industrial period. The extended family structure and the strong kinship ties are viewed as the product of agrarian traditional societies, while the nuclear family is the outcome of modernization (see Plamore, Klein, and Marzuki, 1970). The extended family structure has been described as either an obstacle to or a victim of modernization (Inkeles and Smith, 1974). Therefore, this structure is expected to diminish and even to disappear in the wake of modernization (Goode, 1963). This conclusion is based on the assumption that urbanization,

9

industrialization, and the other factors of modernization exert great pressure on the individual to reduce his intensive kin ties and to become independent. A modern individual emphasizes achievement rather than ascribed values, since economic mobility becomes the result of the individual's effort rather than the extended family support (Levy, 1965; Plamore, Klein, and Marzuki, 1970).

The modernization approach has been used intensively in social studies on Middle Eastern societies. These societies have been viewed as traditional, uniform, and stable (Rosenfeld, 1972). They are presumed to be even more traditional and resistant to modernization than other developing societies because of Islam and the Arab culture (Rosenfeld, 1972). Patai (1983:279-280) noted "in modern Western culture, the new is considered better than the old, and thus change in itself is considered a good; in tradition-bound Arab cultures, the old is regarded as better than the new, and thus the retention of the existing order is considered a good." However, there has always been the hope to change the "changeless Middle East" by the import of modernization and westernization. This "lies in the love-hate relationship with the Christian and the Judaist worlds, and particularly with the Western World" (Pat Caldwell, 1977:603).

The traditional attributes of Middle Eastern societies are reflected in the family structure. The extended family structure has been the ideal family structure in these societies (Good, 1963). The "Arab family" has been described as patrilineal, patrilocal, patriarchal, extended, endogamous, and to some extent polygynous (Patai, 1967; Lutfiyya, 1970). Kinship ties are highly valued. The nuclear family is submerged within the other familial units. The preferred marriage is largely confined to blood kin and is aimed mainly at providing more sons and in turn more male members to the extended family and the kinship groups (see Goode, 1963; Lutfiyya, 1970; Al-Nouri, 1980).

These traditional patterns are expected to be replaced by modern patterns as a result of the modernization process taking place in the Middle East (Gulick, 1968). A similar trend has been noted among Arabs in Israel, and at a more rapid rate. This is basically because of their exposure to the Jewish population who are characterized as the agents of westernization. As Kanaana noted, "the Arab minority in Israel is probably modernizing and changing more rapidly than any other group in the Middle East today. The change is generated through the somewhat sudden and very intensive contact of this previously traditional Middle Eastern peasant agricultural group with a highly modernized and

Westernized society: the Israeli Jewish society" (Kanaana, 1975:6).

These changes are expected to affect specific aspects of family life. The strength of the kinship structure and the extended family is expected to be drastically diminished and replaced by the conjugal family which stresses the immediate interests of the spouses and their children (Avitsour, 1978). Women's status is expected to be strengthened by passing from traditional to transitional or modern patterns. This is expected to be coupled with a change in the traditional roles of women which have been restricted to bearing and rearing children (see Datan, 1972). The process of the "breakdown" of the extended family is expected to continue rapidly and to undermine the basis of the patriarchal system (Arnon and Raviv, 1980).

In addition, the introduction of a democratic political system in local elections, in place of the traditional political system used before the establishment of Israel, is expected to lead ultimately to the replacement of the identification with the kinship group (hamula) by the identification with national leadership and formal organizations (Avitsour, 1978; Layish, 1975).

Along with the modernization process, some scholars have placed emphasis on the fact that the Arab minority in Israel has witnessed increasing inequality and dependence on the Jewish dominant sector (see Rosenfeld, 1964; Smooha, 1980; Lustick, 1980). "The Arabs' economic dependence is reinforced by political subordination. They do not have control of their institutions. Jews run Arab education and mass media, manage the special Arab departments and intervene in Arab local government and state-wide politics. In order to weaken Arab national consciousness and avert national struggle, the Arabs are treated as a mere ethnic group, are denied the status of national minority and even deprived of cultural autonomy" (Smooha, 1978:46). The drastic changes which occurred after the establishment of the State of Israel have affected as well the internal relations among the several groups in the Arab localities. A shift has occurred from the internal dependence of these groups to the external dependence of these groups on the Jewish sector (Al-Haj, 1985). These factors have major repercussions on family life. They constitute a barrier for changing, and to some extent they even reinforce, traditional patterns (Rosenfeld, 1968).

To link our research formulation with the theoretical framework, our major questions are: Is there a typical family lifestyle in Shefar-A'm, or a diversity of types? What is the nature of the relationships among the familial units and between them and the other analytical levels: the individual, group, communal, and societal levels? Do these levels affect family patterns in a uniform or a diverse manner? What are the major changes in the direction of the effects among the different levels, including the family, over time? What is the direction of development in the family patterns of the several groups over time? Have there been changes towards greater similarity or greater diversity? What is the effect of the modernization process on the normative and the behavioral family patterns in a dependent community which has limited or no access to the opportunity structure, but has achieved an advanced stage of individual modernization? What is the effect of the changing group status structure in the community and the modes of internal dependence between the local groups on the family patterns?

Research Methods

When selecting our research methods, we faced the problem of defining the boundaries of the community under research. This point has been noted as a major problem and controversial issue in community studies (see Poplin, 1972; Hillery, 1955). However, most studies agree that several variables have to be taken into consideration when defining community: political administrative boundaries, economic activity, social interaction among the community members, identification with the community, and other psychological elements (Bilsborrow, 1981). Hillery (1971) has emphasized the collective life shared in the community and interaction between community members and the community institutions. In this sense, belonging to a specific community grants the members some benefits (several kinds of services) and protection. But it carries with it several responsibilities as well, such as tax payments, commitment to the community rules, etc. (Findley, 1982).

There are several complementary definitions of a community. They differ depending on the perspective from which the community is viewed. Hillery's definition encompasses several of these points: "community consists of persons in social interaction within a geographic area and having one or more additional common ties" (Hillery, 1955:118). This definition includes territorial bases (geographic), sociological considerations (social interaction), and psychocultural variables (communities) (see Poplin, 1972).

The combination of these elements has also guided our

12

definition of the boundaries of Shefar-A'm. Community affiliation is defined not only by the identification of the community members, but also by the perception of members of other communities. This is particularly important when community members have to be distinguished from members of other communities in the case of specific crucial events. For example, in Shefar-A'm blood vengeance may become a collective responsibility of the community. This is true when the murderer is suspected to be from a certain community but he is not definitely identified. In this case, every member in the community is expected and obligated to seek vengeance for the group of the victim. Sometimes, members have to share the payment of the ransom. Therefore, it becomes of major importance to be aware who is part of the local community.

The territorial element may be an important factor in determining community affiliation. However, this raises the question of how territorial boundaries are defined: Are they determined according to the official definition of jurisdictions, natural boundaries, or other informal factors? In an agrarian community, residence within the confines of the community's lands (agricultural as well as developed areas) is a major indicator of community affiliation (Antoun, 1972). Nobody can live outside the community lands and still be affiliated with it. Yet this does not solve the whole problem. Some people can live on the lands of a given community and still be affiliated with other communities. Therefore, it is useful to add to the territorial variable the duration of residence, the perception of permanence, and formal affiliation. A person can be affiliated with the community if he lives on its lands permanently (actually or perceived), not periodically (Antoun, 1972). Analysis of the case of Shefar-A'm shows that the most important elements of formal affiliation include the right to vote in local elections, the use of community services (water, health, schooling) and religious services, such as marriage registration. The element of tax payment is problematic since there are some dozen Bedouin families who live on the fringes of the locality, receive their services, and vote in Shefar-A'm but pay municipal taxes to Jewish local councils located a distance of about fifteen miles from the locality. Those Bedouin are attached formally to the Jewish councils because they live on an area located outside the Shefar-A'm jurisdiction.

Another factor used in this study is social participation in community affairs. Unlike other studies which have related to social participation in general (see Poplin, 1972) we note that the nature of such participation is the crucial factor, not the

13

participation per se. Since there have been intensive relations among the communities in the region (in particular during the period preceding the establishment of Israel), mutual participation in such events as wedding ceremonies and funerals has been very common. The nature of the participation which distinguishes locals from "guests" can be noticed only by a person who is aware of the cultural habits and rule of the community. For example, in a funeral after the dead is buried, family members stand in a line to be comforted. The "guests," those from outside the community, are given priority to be the first consolers. The leader of the community (or the oldest person) usually invites the "guests" to pass in front of the mourning family and the locals to follow them. In this case it is very easy to identify the community members.

Taking these elements into consideration, we defined the boundaries of Shefar-A'm as including those people who live on Shefar-A'm lands (according to the land registration by the Mandatory Government in 1935), vote in local elections and receive community services, participate in informal social activities as locals not as "guests," and bear responsibility towards the community in the case of collective events. This definition includes a population size larger than that recognized by the Interior Ministry. The formal definition is confined to the municipal jurisdiction. This includes only the ecologically built-up area and may eliminate about one-fourth of the town's population.

The research strategy noted earlier affected the design of our research methods. Family lifestyles are viewed in our study as an integral part of broader contexts and processes in the community and the wider society (see Hugo, 1981; Findley, 1982; McNicoll, 1983; Blau, 1960). Therefore, a mixture of micro and macro methods will be employed. These methods are used in an integrative way, in the sense that each reveals a part of the picture, while the combination of them covers the picture as a whole (see Caldwell, Reddy, and Caldwell, 1982). Our analysis considers the contextual factors in the community but further relates to the community as a network of social interaction at several levels that includes interaction between individuals, individuals and groups, groups and groups, and the community as a whole and the external environment (see Poplin, 1972). Hence, a synthesis between qualitative and quantitative methods will be employed in order to cover the community-level variables and to construct an in-depth picture about the dynamics of the interaction at the different levels. Our study attempts to develop a comprehensive picture about the current family patterns and to trace the changes in these patterns retrospectively. This aim necessitates the use of longitudinal methods covering family patterns at different periods. In addition, the social history of the community is viewed as an integral part of current processes and an important component of the explanatory variables (see Allman, 1978). This necessitates the use of historical documents and other supplementary methods, in particular conversations with aged informants.

In order to meet these needs, a synthesis of historical, socio-anthropological, and demographic methods were employed. Our field study, which lasted three years (1979-1982), included the following methodological approaches: we analyzed a large number of documents including formal registration, official papers and private diaries and other personal documents. This was the initial approach by which we started to explore the several aspects of the community: the social history of the several religious groups and subgroups, their background, and the formation of their social status as well as their relations with the neighboring population outside the community. The analysis of the private diaries and documents provided an in-depth picture about life histories of several families from the different groups. The official documents were obtained from the archives of the municipality, the state archives, the records of the employment bureau, the local laborers council, and documents of the *Mukhtars*[2] (informal community leaders who handled the religious affairs of various groups until the establishment of Israel). More specifically, these documents included land registration and land holdings according to the households and the religious groups in different periods since 1914, land designation, land sales, and confiscations since 1935, population movements, population size and distribution according to age, sex (this is restricted to the post-1948 period), several municipal and governmental services, the employment situation since 1910, stores, businesses and other economic branches, the struggle over the local power system through the municipal elections since 1915, marriage and divorce registrations, and other subjects.

The private documents and diaries were obtained from residents of Shefar-A'm and from the surrounding communities.

----

[2] We have followed the system of International Phonetic Association (IPA) in the translation of Arabic words and names.

They included, among other things, reports about economic activities, social activities, relations between the family members and among the kinship group, informal relationships between members of the religious groups, births, deaths, and migration along with specific dates in the community including the establishment of the municipal council in 1910, the murder of Ṣaleh Affendi (landowner from El-Makir) in 1933, the hostilities between the Moslems and the Druze in 1939, the capture of Shefar-A'm by the Israeli forces on the 14th of July 1948, and the internal refugee movements in the 1950s.

The private documents were classified into two groups. The first contained personal data, reflected in the reports of individuals about their own experience or reflected in their correspondence with officials. The second contained reports of several communal activities written by people who witnessed or participated in the activities. The second group of documents was obtained from prominent persons in the community: leaders, large landowners, teachers, and persons from prominent families.

One set of unique diaries was obtained from a prominent Christian family, covering a period of about one century, 1882-1975. Three persons were involved in the writing of these diaries: the grandfather who died in the 1920s, the father who died in the 1960s, and the son aged then about 80 years. The diaries included day-to-day reports about family affairs as well as the main community matters: the weather; occupational situation; prices of vegetables, foodstuffs, and other items; social events in the community, relations among the religious groups; and other interesting issues.

During the field work many unexpected materials were collected. We experienced a process of "chain information" in which almost every person from whom we obtained documents indicated other people who might have documents of interest. This proved to be of great importance. The experience with municipal documents was remarkable. At the beginning we found only documents relating to the period after the establishment of Israel. The interview with the former mayor (Jabūr Jabūr), who served in this position over 36 years (1933-1969), was particularly useful. He revealed that the municipal council was located for a specific period in the old castle of the town (el-Qala). Our assumption that documents might be found in that abandoned building was confirmed. We found a wooden box which contained hundreds of documents about the various activities and services of the municipality from its establishment.

In addition to these documents we carried out a

comprehensive survey covering all the families of school children at all educational levels from kindergarten through high school. The data were derived from the enrollment cards of the pupils and covered 1,765 families. Clearly the survey was selective. It obviously excluded the families with no school age children. But the survey collected detailed statistical data for two-thirds of the families in Shefar-A'm. About 80 percent of the population was covered because families with children in school are larger on average than the other families. This survey provided a comprehensive picture of the basic characteristics of the families among the several groups in terms of number of children per family, spacing between children within the family, parents' age, education, employment, kinship relationship before marriage, residential structure of the family, and related elements. The data from the enrollment cards were recorded by the school secretaries and some of the teachers. Only one pupil was chosen from each household to prevent duplications.

To compensate for some of the biases inherent in school surveys, a more comprehensive survey was undertaken. This survey consisted of 240 detailed open-ended interviews with a cross section of the married population. The survey covered 120 married couples in the town: local Moslems, local Christians, local Druze, immigrant Moslems, and Druze El-Jabal. The sample was selected from the official voting register of the population in the town, which included all the population aged 18 and over. Only married people were selected and the population was subdivided into three main groups -- Moslems, Christians, and Druze. Among each group a random number of names were selected according to its percentage of the town population: 47 Moslems, 43 Christians, and 30 Druze. Immigrant groups (internal refugees, Bedouins and Druze El-Jabal) were included among the religious groups. Men and women were interviewed along with their spouses. (In two cases the spouses were not available and they were omitted). The interviews were conducted in an informal atmosphere and focused on a wide range of topics about family lifestyles. Each interview lasted 4 to 5 hours and several spanned two meetings. All the interviews with men were conducted by the researcher. The interviews with women were conducted by female interviewers, because of the sensitivity of several questions, mainly about contraceptive practices and family planning. In addition to the detailed interviews, we conducted some semi-structured conversations with both spouses together. This method had some limitations. Since women were usually influenced by their husbands, the women reported attitudes about specific family

17

issues which differed completely from those reported in interviews where the spouses were separated.

In addition, it was difficult to conduct such conversations with traditional families. This method did have some advantages. During these conversations we could notice, to some extent, the nature of the relations between the spouses. In some cases they also reminded each other about important points. However, we applied this method only in a few interviews because the limitations exceeded the advantages.

Although the questionnaire was structured and a specific set of questions were asked to all the respondents, we had some flexibility. Sometimes we added different questions in order to clarify a specific point. Throughout the interviews we tried to direct the respondents to the main questions. In some cases this was difficult, particularly in interviews with old people who tended to give general answers or to note several issues which were not connected with the subject.

In the vast majority of the interviews the respondents were highly cooperative. We had some difficulties only in two cases. The first was with a Moslem interviewee who refused to be interviewed during the fasting month of the Moslems (ramadan). We interviewed him later after the fasting month was over. The second was with a Druze interviewee who lived, during our study, in a temporary house in the fields outside the town. The husband refused to cooperate at the beginning. Later we were informed by his son that the father did not want to "waste his time in answering questions out of his interest, especially when he is busy in harvesting". We waited until the harvest season was over and the family returned to their permanent house in the town where we conducted the interview without any problems. It should be noted that we tried to conduct all the interviews without the presence of other people, whether family members or friends. In most cases this was possible, but in a few cases the presence of other people was unavoidable. We usually asked these outsiders not to intervene during the interview, though this was not always the case.

A survey focusing on family planning services was also carried out. These data were obtained from the records of the local family planning clinic. The survey covered all 685 women who attended and received birth control through the clinic, throughout its existence from 1976 until 1981. The local women were selected from a larger list which included women from other communities as well, since the clinic served five neighboring villages and the nearby Bedouins, in addition to the Shefar-A'm

18

population. The records obtained from the clinic included information about the following points: religious affiliation, age, number of pregnancies, number of surviving children and their ages, number of children who died before they were five years old, abortions and detailed data about their history of contraceptive use.

The nurses in the family planning clinic were very helpful. They provided unwritten information which was not included in the records such as: the role of husbands in family planning, the kinds of traditional contraception practiced by women before they came to the clinic, differences in the contraceptive regulations between women from the several religious groups, and other related issues. The nurses drew our attention to the internal survey they conducted in the clinic about the sources which affected the women's decision to practice family planning. These informal data raised several points which had not been considered at the beginning.

For the marriage analysis we collected data covering a period of fifty years, 1931-1981. Information concerning all the 2,351 marriages conducted in the community was obtained from the reports of the clergy who performed the marriage ceremonies for each of the three religious groups. When we started to classify the cases in these reports according to kinship group affiliation, some of them were unclear. The clergy drew our attention to some points which had to be cautiously handled. These included cases where the names of the bride and the groom were not precisely or fully reported. Only the father's name was mentioned, not the hamula name. In addition, some reported the spouse's hamula name after marriage and thus the information about the relationship before marriage was lacking. In order to handle this problem, we selected all these names with the help of the clergy and obtained the full, accurate names before marriage from the population registration department in the municipality. The director of the department was very helpful, since he had been working in the municipality over twenty years and was highly aware of the family names in the community.

Detailed interviews with community leaders and professionals were also conducted. The initial assessment of our findings revealed that group affiliation and group cohesion play an important role in community life, particularly in the social and the political involvement of the individuals in the community (for similar findings see Blau, 1960). In this sense, it became clear that community leaders exert a great influence. Their life experience enriched our analysis and provided an in-depth picture.

Therefore, we decided to conduct detailed interviews with some of the prominent community leaders of the different groups. Nine detailed interviews were conducted: two with Moslem leaders, two with Christian leaders, two with Druze leaders and one with each of the prominent leaders of refugees, Bedouins and Druze El-Jabal. It was much easier to identify the leaders who served in official positions (such as the mayor and the secretary of the Laborers Council) than unofficial leaders. However, during the municipal elections it was abundantly clear who were the important leaders of the community, who could represent their groups and affect the decision making among them.

The interviews were semi-structured and related to the current situation of the community as well as each leader's interpretation of past events and the changes in the local power system. In addition to the common questions, every leader was asked a different set of questions according to his position and the kind of activities in which he had been involved.

In addition to the leadership interviews, some interviews with professionals were conducted. These professionals were familiar with family affairs, in particular family planning and contraception, and included three physicians, two nurses (one in the family planning clinic and the other in the Infant Welfare Center-Tipat Halav), and one social worker. These interviews supported first hand reports from the interviewees' own experience. One of the interviews was conducted with a local physician who came to Shefar-A'm from Lebanon in 1947 to work in his own clinic in the locality. During the 1950s and until the mid-1960s, he was the only physician in the whole region and served all the population in the surrounding villages. The sharing of his wide experience contributed a great deal to our data. Since he was the first physician in the region to be active in formal programs of family planning, he talked in detail about his experience and the changing response of the several groups to contraceptive use over time. Some of his personal documents about this issue were also useful.

Participant observation and conversation with informants were used throughout our field study. One of the advantages of this method was that we were not restricted to a specific set of questions, although the patterns we intended to focus on were very clear. Continuous observation was made possible by the researchers participation in community activities in the different fields and by informal visits to many families in the locality.

The conversations with informants ranged over different aspects of family life and the community. Older informants from the different groups, both men and women, were particularly helpful. The information obtained was useful in reconstructing family lifestyles for the pre-1948 period. However, we treated the reports of the informants cautiously by comparing them thoroughly with the other data sources. Unlike the anthropological approach which may rely heavily on participant observation and informants (see Poplin, 1972), these methods were used in our research as supplementary sources. The findings obtained from these methods were combined with the findings of our main data sources noted above. This approach contributed to the validity of the data and to an in-depth understanding of the reality behind the numbers and the statistics.

In sum, throughout our field study we adopted a diverse strategy combining different historical, socio-anthropological, and demographic methods. These methods were used simultaneously and the several sources were compared with each other in order to enhance the validity and the reliability of our data. Our study synthesizes micro and macro approaches. These approaches are supplementary rather than contradictory. In this sense, the document analysis furnished the basis for a better understanding of the data obtained from the comprehensive survey; the combination of both methods provided a solid base for the design of the sample of the detailed interviews and the questions included in the questionnaire. Each of the other data sources covered a specific set of related points. In addition, when combined with other sources, a better understanding of the whole picture emerges.

Our findings were continuously assessed throughout the several stages of the field study, rather than being delayed until the end of the field work. This had several advantages. It enabled us to increase the efficiency of the several sources, to add questions and several appropriate variables throughout the research, and to direct the different methods according to our study interests. Despite the fact that the general framework of our study was clear from the very beginning, we did not adopt a closed strategy. A considerable part of our findings emerged only during the field work. Therefore, some methods were added to our core methods in order to meet the emerging needs.

2

Shefar-A'm: Demographic, Economic, and Group Status Structure

Contextual factors, which include the economic, cultural, social, and political structures of the community, have been emphasized as crucial for an in-depth understanding of the several aspects of family lifestyles (see Blau, 1960; Davis, Speath, and Huston, 1961; Hugo, 1981; Findley, 1982). Analysis confined to individual variables has been found to be incomplete in large part because the family is not isolated from the surrounding environment which exerts a significant influence on family decision making. Therefore, combining individual level and community level variables was noted as the best analytic strategy (see Hugo, 1981).

Our analysis considers both contextual and individual factors, but we further view the community as a dynamic network of interaction. In this sense we adopt the approach taken by community action theory, which emphasizes the interaction between individuals and between various groups and institutions of which the community is composed (see Poplin, 1972). This leads to the analysis of the community's horizontal and vertical axes. The horizontal axis involves the relationship of individuals to individuals or of groups to groups within the locality; the vertical axis involves the relationship of the individual to a local interest group and of that interest group to a general state or national organization (see Warren, 1956; Poplin, 1972:17).

In this chapter we will analyze systematically the demographic, economic, and group status structure in Shefar-A'm for several periods. Demographic structure includes: the main components of population growth, changes in population movement, and the changing demographic balance among the main groups in the community. In terms of economic structure we will examine: the modes of production, the occupational structure, and the changing economic dependency among the groups in the community, and between the community and the external environment. All these elements will furnish the basis for our analysis of the structure of group status within the community. This includes the community power system and the nature of the social interaction between the several groups. Our chief questions will be: What is the main stratification system in Shefar-A'm? What is the nature of the linkage between this system and group affiliation? What are the repercussions of the demographic elements, modes of economic dependency, group relationships outside the community, and modernization changes on the local power system and on the nature of the interaction between individuals and groups within the community?

Demographic Structure

Shefar-A'm is located on the western fringes of Lower Galilee, in the center of a triangle approximately 18 kilometers from Acre, Haifa, and Nazareth. In the early 1980s it had an estimated population of 22,000 and was the second largest Arab town in Israel. During the Ottoman period, until 1918, Shefar-A'm served as a district center (mūdiriyyah) and provided services to 22 villages in the region. As a result it was the first settlement in the northern part of the country officially to be declared a town.

As a service center Shefar-A'm attracted many immigrants who settled there during the various periods. An analysis of the settlement's nucleus shows that Druze and a number of well-to-do Christian families were among the first settlers. There was, however, considerable population movement among the Christians, some of whom emigrated to Lebanon but returned later during the eighteenth century. During this same period, and in particular under the rule of Dahar al-Omar (1698-1775), Moslem families began to settle in Shefar-A'm, especially on the eastern fringes of the built-up area. Throughout the Ottoman and British Mandatory Periods, the Christian community preserved its numeric preponderance (approximately 45 percent), while the Moslems constituted the second largest community (approximately 38 percent), and the Druze the smallest (17 percent).

Following the establishment of the State of Israel in 1948, drastic changes took place in Shefar-A'm's demographic and social

24

structure. These changes were partly due to the massive evacuation of local families who became refugees in neighboring Arab countries, and partly due to the reshuffling of populations within Israeli borders (what became known in the wake of the war as a "green line") as the result of official government policy.

In the first months of 1948 Shefar-A'm had a population of 4,869. Following the war, the sociodemographic structure of the local community radically changed when large sections of the Moslem population, as well as a number of Christian and Druze families, left the town after they learned that the Israeli Army intended to capture it. Many fled to the east, to Ṣafūrieh, and to the north, to the Jodpata region in Galilee, while other Moslem families crossed the border into Lebanon. After the capture of Shefar-A'm on July 14, 1948, when it became known that it was possible to return and to receive an Israeli identity card, dozens of families returned, although a smaller number went further north and settled in Lebanon perhaps expecting the situation would clear up.

During the next three years there followed a fluctuating situation of immigration and emigration. Some families were reunited with returning relatives who settled again in Shefar-A'm and became Israeli citizens, while other families were split because the authorities did not permit the return of their members who had left the town during the war (see also Segev, 1984). It was almost exclusively the Moslem families that were broken up in this manner.

A comparison of the population before and after Israeli independence (1948) shows that 494 inhabitants--474 Moslems and 20 Christians--left Shefar-A'm for Arab countries. No Druze left the settlement permanently. Those among the Druze who had left at the beginning of the war returned immediately and none of them was refused an Israeli identity card (that is, citizenship) by the Military Government. On the other hand, there also was a population influx into Shefar-A'm during these first three years: 548 refugees from neighboring villages which had been destroyed during the war moved to the town. This inmigration balanced the outmigration. In 1953 the population had become more or less stabilized and was composed as shown in Table 2.1. More significant changes in the demographic structure of the town population have taken place since the early 1950s. This is because of the natural increase and the inmigration of refugees, Bedouin and Druze El-Jabal.

Figure 1 indicates that natural increase was the most important factor in population growth. Two main patterns may be

TABLE 2.1

SHEFAR-A'M POPULATION BY RELIGIOUS GROUP, 1953

Population Groups	Communities			Total
	Christians	Moslems	Druze	
Locals	2216	1192	958	4366
Refugees	120	428	–	548
Total	2336	1620	958	4914
Percentage of total	47.51	32.97	19.52	100.0

Figure 1. Rate of Population Increase in Shefar-A'm by Group and Source of Increase (1947-1981)

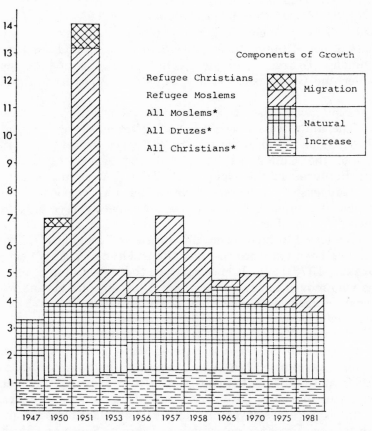

*All includes refugee and native natural increase.

	1947	1950	1951	1953	1956	1957	1958	1965	1970	1975	1981
Rate of Net Migration		3.2	10.3	1.02	.63	2.79	1.66	.26	1.0	1.1	0.8
Rate of Natural Increase	3.3	3.8	3.8	4.1	4.2	4.3	4.3	4.5	4.0	3.75	3.4
Total Annual Increase	3.3	7.0	14.1	5.12	4.83	7.09	5.96	4.76	5.0	4.85	4.2

observed: rapid increase reaching the highest rate at the mid-1960s, and a slow but consistent increase from the mid-60s to the 80s. The crude birth rate in 1954 was 48.1 per 1,000 among Moslems (compared to 48.8 per 1,000 among Moslems in the whole country), 34.6 per 1,000 among Christians (33.6), and 48.1 per 1,000 among Druze (48.0). There was a significant increase in the birth rate during the second decade, in the 1960s, with rates of 57.9 per 1,000 among Moslems (57.3 in the total country), 35.4 among Christians (33.7), and 49.7 among the Druze (43.0). The birth rate decreased in the 1980s but it still remained relatively high: 38.9 per 1,000 among the Moslems (37.5), 24.3 per 1,000 among Christians (19.9), and 38.1 per 1,000 among Druze (35.0) (for country wide statistics see, Friedlander and Goldscheider, 1984; Statistical Abstract of Israel, 1983).

Migration was also a considerable source of population growth. The main waves occurred during the early and the late 1950s because of the influx of internal refugees to the town. the definition of the United Nations Relief and Works Agency for Palestine Refugees in the Near East (UNRWA) to define Arab internal refugees: "A person whose normal residence was Palestine for a minimum of two years immediately preceding the outbreak of the conflict in 1948 and who, as a result of this conflict has lost his home and his means of livelihood". This definition has been extended to cover the children of such a person (see Barakat, 1973:147). It encompasses the Palestinian external refugees who moved to several neighboring Arab countries as well as internal refugees who moved to other localities within Israel, including Shefar-A'm.

Examination of the stages of the movement and settlement of internal refugees in Shefar-A'm reveals three main periods: the search for asylum, 1948-1951; waiting and expectations, 1952-1957; and stable settlement, since 1957. About 50 percent of the refugees moved to the town directly from neighboring Arab villages which were destroyed during the 1948 war: Meār, Waart Sarris, Kasāyer, Ūm El-zeināt, Ruweis, Damūn, Sasa, and Hoshé (all these villages are located in the western Galilee at a distance of between 2 to 10 miles from Shefar-A'm). In most cases flight occurred during battle conditions. The immediate goal of flight was to reach a place of asylum. The refugees were not prepared to face such sudden events and very few knew what to do, since they lacked social and political organizations (see also Sayigh, 1979).

The refugees perceived their situation as temporary. They

expected their problem to be solved and to return to their homes. But as time passed without the refugees being able to exert any control over political and other events, hope decreased. As one refugee noted, "rāhat el-sakra uejat el-fikra" (the shock was over and thought took place). In the late 1950s, refugees began to plan for a longer term settlement. By 1958 they began to purchase lands and to build their houses. In addition, during the third period a second wave of refugee movement occurred. About 35 percent of the refugees moved to the town during the period 1958-1961, and about 15 percent moved after 1961. As a result, some original communities and kinship groups were reunited. In 1980, refugees constituted about 22 percent of the town's population: 36 percent of the Moslem population and only 8 percent of the Christian (see Al-Haj, 1985).

Another group within Shefar-A'm are the Bedouin who settled in the town's fields. Members of the large Bedouin tribes, such as the Turkmān, Sawaid and Hujāirāt, then used the fields for grazing. Permanent Bedouin settlements on Shefar-A'm land began in the early twentieth century. According to a report of 1917, 89 Bedouin families lived there. Several documents indicate that the Bedouin had intensive relationships with the Shefar-A'm population, both socially and in terms of economic relationships.

Although the Bedouin maintained close contact with Shefar-A'm for several decades, their permanent settlement in the town did not begin until the 1950s. The migration waves came from two directions. The first was a gradual and slow influx of Bedouin from the immediately surrounding region, while the second was an influx of Bedouin families from distant regions in the north. The first wave of Bedouin settlers came in 1954 and consisted of 100 persons, most of whom settled in the southern part of the town, while the others settled in the eastern part (Golani and Katz, 1963). The second wave took place in 1958 when 34 families, numbering 241 persons, came.

These Bedouin tended to settle on the fringes of the town and were not formally under the municipality's jurisdiction; for this reason they were neither granted voting rights in municipal elections, nor entitled to municipal services such as water and electricity. However, in 1967 the Bedouin settlement came under the municipal jurisdiction of Shefar-A'm. Since then additional Bedouin families have come to join their relatives who have lived there since the 1950s. The Bedouin presently account for 6.5 percent of the total population, and 13 percent of the Moslem community.

The third main group of in-migrants are the Druze. "Druze

El-Jabal", or "El-Hawarńe" as the local Druze call them, originally came as soldiers with Sakhib El-Wahhāb, the Syrian commander who led Arab armies in the Galilee during the 1948 war. On May 24, 1948, Sakhib El-Wahhāb returned to Syria with most of his soldiers. Approximately 100 soldiers, almost all of them Druze, stayed behind. At the end of the war they volunteered for service in the Israeli Army, within the framework of the Mahal ("volunteers from abroad"). Most of them subsequently married other Druze and settled in various places throughout Israel. In 1957, 30 of these Druze families settled in Shefar-A'm mainly in a special neighborhood for released soldiers that was built by the Defense Ministry in 1958.

Since that time the local inhabitants have called them "El-Hawarńe" because of their origin in the Hūrān, but the settlers call themselves "Druze El-Jabal". The difference between these two names is more than semantic, it is an expression of the delicate relations between the Druze settlers and the other inhabitants, and in particular between the settlers and the members of the local Druze community. These relations, as will be discussed later, are characterized by majority-minority asymmetric relations. The name "El-Hawarńe", which bears a negative meaning, reinforces the local Druze's prejudice of the in-migrant Druze.

Economic Structure: Before the Establishment of Israel

Until the last years of the British Mandate (late 1940s), Shefar-A'm was an agricultural settlement. The administrative centrality of the town resulted, among other things, in the control of large plots of land by its population. Until land registration was introduced by the Mandatory Government in 1933, the population of Shefar-A'm had approximately 125,000 *dunam* or 500 acres (see definition under table 2.2) Most of the lands were musha, collective tenure of a land area. The land was redistributed among the three religious groups every five years. Each group received its share according to its size and the duration of settlement in the town. Christians controlled about one-half of the land, while the second half was divided between the Druze and eight Moslem households. Moslems received the smallest portion, due to the fact that they were the last settlers (Table 2.2). Following the land registration, about 30,000 dunam were declared government land, allegedly because they consisted of uncultivated hill country, while about 7,000 dunam were sold to

TABLE 2.2

LAND OWNERSHIP IN SHEFAR-A'M BY RELIGIOUS
GROUP AND SIZE OF HOLDING,
1935[1]

Ownership by Household	Christians	Moslems	Druze
Less than one Fadan (small plots)	47.0	78.0	40.0
1-2 Fadans (modest plots)	17.0	18.0	20.0
2 Fadans and over (large plots)	36.0	4.0	40.0
Total	100.0	100.0	100.0
Percentage of land ownership by group	50.0	12.0	38.0

[1]Abramovitch and Gilpat (1940) write that the Palestinian Fadan is not a fixed surface unit, but varies from region to region. It is always and everywhere a plot large enough to sustain an average fellah family under the specific conditions prevailing in the region. In Shefar-A'm one Fadan is 250 dunam.

Bedouin and Jews by Ṣaleh Affendi, a wealthy landowner from Acre. One of the immediate results of the registration was the breakdown of communal land, or the musha system, as had happened in other parts of Palestine as well (Waschitz, 1947; Stein, 1984). Most of the remaining land became mulk, privately-owned land. Approximately 32,000 dunam of this area consisted of cultivated agricultural land.

In an agrarian society, the control of land, and in particular of agricultural land, is not only a means of existence, but also a status symbol and an instrument of power in other spheres. It is therefore important to understand how the land was divided among and within the various religious groups. Detailed analysis of documents of land registration derived from Shefar-A'm municipality and the Mukhtars of each religious group revealed the data presented in Table 2.2. From Table 2.2 we may draw a number of important conclusions:

1. The percentage of families subsisting by cultivating their own land without additional employment was high among the Druze and the Christians and low among Moslems (53 percent, 60 percent, and 22 percent, respectively).

2. Two broader categories can be clearly distinguished among the local population: those with and those without land. Only a relatively thin layer of the population belongs to a third category, the middle class: 22 percent of the Druze, 17 percent of the Christians, and 18 percent of the Moslems. These families were generally able to sustain themselves without the help of hired labor, except occasionally during the harvest.

3. Class and group boundaries do not overlap completely. Each religious group is not a class, but instead comprises several classes. As in Lebanon and other Middle Eastern countries class division and religious affiliation do not coincide (see Chevallier, 1971).

Analysis of land ownership by each religious group revealed that Christians were the most dominant economically. They possessed 50 percent of the land, although they accounted for only 45 percent of the population. The Druze had the largest portion of land in proportion to their numbers: 17 percent of the population with 38 percent of the land. The Moslems were at the bottom of the scale: they controlled only 12 percent of thee cultivated land, although they constituted 38 percent of the population.

Agriculture

A governmental committee reported that during the Mandatory Period, 86 percent of Moslems and 73 percent of Christians in Palestine worked in agriculture (Rosenfeld, 1962). A similar picture emerges in Shefar-A'm--90 percent of Druze households, 80 percent of Moslems and about 70 percent of the Christians were engaged in agriculture. 65 percent of the households worked their own land, 19 percent were compelled to work as hired labor in addition to working their own land, while 11 percent had no land of their own and made their living mainly as employed agricultural workers. Among the last mentioned were farmhands, shepherds and casual laborers. In addition to working as hired laborers they often also tilled a small plot of land they had received or leased from their employer. Five percent were employed as camel drivers and transported the agricultural products from the fields to the threshing floor.

In Shefar-A'm, like other agricultural areas in Palestine, agriculture was extensive, with two main seasons, winter and summer. Grains constituted the main crop of the peasants. Most of the production was for their own consumption and for taxes--little went to the markets (see Horowitz and Hinden, 1938; Rosenfeld, 1964). Nevertheless, Shefar A'm differed from other places in the sense that most of the large landowners were locals--not city dwellers (for comparison see Waschitz, 1947). Land owners emerged as distinctive social class in Shefar-A'm. They hired wage labor from the locality as well as from the neighboring villages, mainly during the harvest seasons.

The main crops were wheat, barley, sesame, and watermelon. Analysis of documents revealed that about 36 percent of the wheat, 30 percent of the barley, 50 percent of the sesame, and about 70 percent of the watermelon went to the market. These figures are somewhat higher than the average in the country as a whole (see Abramovitch and Gelphat, 1944:25). Evidence from some diaries of local peasants showed that throughout the months of July to September, camel drivers were hired to transfer the crops from the town to the nearby cities, Acre and Haifa.

Trade and Industry

Trade and industry were important branches in the employment structure of Shefar-A'm. Towards the end of the

Ottoman period, at the turn of the century, about 15 percent of the households made their living in these two branches. During the British Mandate (until the late 1940s), there was a minor recession in industry, crafts, and trade. An analysis of the employment structure in 1940 shows that 13 percent of the population were engaged in these two branches: 21 percent of the Christians, 8 percent of the Moslems and only 4 percent of the Druze. The central economic position of Shefar-A'm among the surrounding villages and its function as supplier of services made the control of trade and industry an extremely important asset. The local population, and those in the surrounding villages were therefore dependent on the Christians in Shefar-A'm who controlled these two branches.

Analysis of municipal documents of Shefar-A'm revealed that in 1910 there were 11 workshops; they declined to four in 1947. This decline was the result of changes in the administrative status of the town during the Mandatory Period. There were also 10 dairies in 1914, they increased to 19 in 1947. The milk for these dairies was supplied by the Bedouin who settled in scattered locations around the town. In addition, there was one weaving mill and six workshops for soapmaking. All the workshops were small, based on domestic labor. Several hired laborers for specific periods.

In 1911 there were 67 stores in the town. The number increased to 73 stores in 1921 and 84 stores in 1947. Most of these were grocery shops. Detailed data on the types of shops show that there was specialization in the trade and the services in the town, unlike the villages where different services were put together in a small store. The average number of grocery shops was relatively high. In 1921, for example, 31 grocery shops served a population of 2,200 people, for an average of 71 persons per shop. Examination of the available client lists from that period revealed that these shops served the local population as well as the surrounding villages. A decline occurred in the proportion of grocery shops per capita. In 1947 there were 4,700 people and 38 grocery shops, for an average of about 124 persons per shop. A similar picture emerges from the comparison of other service stores (e.g., carpentry, locksmithy, oil press, etc.) between the first and last years of the Mandatory Period. This reflects the decrease in the economic dependency between Shefar-A'm and the neighboring villages.

Analysis of available accounts from the stores revealed that trade was mostly on a monetary basis, not on an exchange basis. However, some peasants bought their supplies throughout the year and paid only after the harvest, because of a money shortage. In some cases, a large part of the crop was spent to pay such debts.

In addition to the retail trade, there was also a wholesale trade--once a week in the "cattle market" and daily in the "vegetable market". It was difficult to document this kind of trade, but informants reported that peasants from Shefar-A'm and the surrounding villages were involved. Documents obtained from the municipality indicated that during the spring stock breeders from Lebanon and Southern Syria came with their cattle to the natural pastures near Shefar-A'm and took part in the "cattle market". The wholesale trade constituted only an additional income for the people involved. The overwhelming majority were originally peasants.

In Shefar-A'm, the process of proletarianization was rather slow compared with the rest of Palestine. Until the late 1930s only a few Shefar-A'm residents worked as employed laborers in other than agricultural work. Towards the end of the 1930s and in the early 1940s the first signs of this process began to appear. On the basis of municipal reports and interviews, we estimate that 10 percent of the wage-earners were employed in non-agricultural work at this time. The majority of this labor force was recruited from among the Moslem community, which was already, at that early date, becoming a reservoir of hired labor.

Several factors combined to cause the delay in the proletarianization process in Shefar-A'm. The surplus labor force, mainly among the Moslems, was absorbed by the large farms of the Christians and the Druze, since most of the landowners in Shefar-A'm were locals and retained their lands. Excluding Şaleh Affendi, almost nobody sold lands to people outside the town. Moreover, the continuity of the extended family among the Druze, even after the death of the patriarch, resulted in the integrity of the land system among this group. This increased the efficiency in agricultural work. In addition, the Jewish settlement, which absorbed some of the Arab labor force in agriculture and construction, was less developed in the Galilee relative to other regions in Palestine (see Rosenfeld, 1964; Soffer, 1981). This decreased work opportunities outside the town. In addition to agriculture, the local trade and industry provided work for a considerable part of the labor force.

In sum, the employment structure and the possession of land during the period prior to the establishment of the State of Israel indicate that there were four main socioeconomic strata, each linked to a religious group. The merchants and business owners

35

were nearly all Christians; the large landowners were mainly Christians and Druze; small farmers were found among all three communities; while the overwhelming majority of the poor peasants (fallāhin) and hired workers were Moslems. This economic structure suggests two patterns of dependence. On the local level, Druze and Christians held the central positions, the former in agriculture, the latter in both agriculture and trade and industry. The Moslems lived along the periphery and were economically dependent on the other two groups. They supplied the unskilled labor force, and only a small percentage of Moslem families could subsist on privately-owned independent farms. On the regional level, the surrounding Arab villages were also dependent on Shefar -A'm, which provided the village population with seasonal agricultural work, maintained trade relations with them and supplied various services to the fallāhin. In this respect, the Christian community was the dominant group.

Economic Patterns after the Establishment of Israel

The occupational structure since the establishment of Israel has been drastically changed to wage labor completely dependent on the Jewish sector. Nevertheless, scholars differ in their assessment of the main stages in this occupational transformation. Israely (1976:232-233) suggested four main stages: 1953-1962, the beginning of change from agricultural to non-agricultural occupation outside the villages; 1963-1966, a rapid increase in the demand for an Arab labor force in the Jewish sector; 1966-1967, a recession; and 1967 and beyond, an economic tide in Israel and the increasing demand for an Arab labor force. Ginat (1981:7) suggested a transitional period, 1948-1953, characterized by high unemployment in the Arab villages. The division suggested by Rosenfeld (1958:71) is completely different. He argues that the occupational transformation of Arabs began in the Mandatory Period, with the Jewish immigration to Palestine in the 1920s and the growing work opportunities outside the Arab localities. The second stage began mainly during World War II, when the British Mandatory Government provided wider occupational opportunities. After the establishment of Israel, there was a rapid continuity of the proletarianization process.

Examination of the occupational structure (Table 2.3) in Shefar-A'm after the establishment of Israel suggests two main periods of occupational transformation: a transitional period (1948-1958) in which several involuntary factors led to the

36

TABLE 2.3

LABOR FORCE AGED 15 AND OVER BY BRANCH OF EMPLOYMENT
AND LOCALITY OF WORK IN SHEFAR-A'M, 1957

Branch of Employment	Number	Percent
Locally Employed		
Agriculture and cattle breeding	514	52.5
Public institutions and education	52	5.3
Construction	50	5.0
Trade and industry	141	14.4
Employment Outside		
Unstable wage labor in agriculture and construction	223	22.8
Total	980	100.0

relative continuity of the previous economic structure, and a rapid process of proletarianization and dependency on the dominant Jewish sector (1959-present). As a result, the occupational structure witnessed an ebb and flow, according to the economic situation in the Jewish sector.

The changes which occurred in the first period furnished the basis for the drastic occupational transformation in the second period. As anticipated, most of the refugees moved to the town during the first decade after the establishment of Israel (the transitional period). They settled without any property. Therefore, they had to compete with the local population within the local poor economic system. This induced directly and indirectly the proletarianization process and the search for wage labor outside the town. The main land confiscations took place in the first period: "the Arab mass flight and the restrictions employed on the movement of those who remained in the country, created a difficult problem: large plots of Arab lands in the country wide were abandoned. Orchards, olive trees and lands which were prepared for planting were deserted..." *(Report of the Ministry of Minorities - 1948-49* :17). This situation was exploited by the Israeli government for mass land confiscations. Several regulations were employed for this purpose concerning uncultivated land, security zones, absentee property, and others.

Analysis of municipal documents regarding Shefar-A'm lands revealed that during the period 1948-1958, 34,518 dunams (36 percent of the lands) were confiscated by several governmental authorities, while 4,000 dunams were confiscated later. In addition to confiscations, land sale constituted an important factor in the decrease of land. About 11,455 dunams were sold to the Bedouins who settled around the town. Currently, the total land area (agricultural as well as non-agricultural) owned by the population of the town is 35,329 dunams, which constitutes only 37 percent of pre-1948 Shefar-A'm lands (Map 1).

Most of the land confiscations were made possible by the absentee regulations. According to these regulations, a person who is a legal owner of property in the area under the law of the State of Israel is considered an absentee if after November 29, 1947 he:

(a) became a citizen in Lebanon, Egypt, Syria, Saudia, Trans Jordan, Iraq, or Yemen; or

(b) lives in one of these countries or in any area of Eretz Israel (Palestine) out of the Israeli law; or

38

(c) was a citizen in Eretz Israel (Palestine) and left his regular residence in the town or village and did not receive a certificate from the custodian on the absentee property to prove that he is not an absentee... *(The Report of the Minorities Ministry, 1948-1949* :8).

However, despite the loss land of Shefar-A'm, about 32 percent of the landowners in the 1950s had plots which were considered large (50 dunams and over), about 26 percent had modest plots (31-49 dunams) and 42 percent had small plots (1-30 dunams), or were landless.[1] This was due to the fact that the Druze lands were less affected by confiscations because they did not move away as a result of the 1948 war. In addition, the continuity of the extended family among the Druze contributed to the land integrity.

During the transitional period, in addition to the control over the movement of the Arab population by the military administration, control was also exerted over commerce, so that the labor force moved outside the locality. Tight control over agricultural production was instituted with the "order of the food control" (1950). Through this, the farmer was allowed to take from his production only what he needed for his own consumption. Any excess was purchased according to "government prices", which was much lower than market prices. This reduced the desirability of agricultural work.

During the early 1950s, the Israeli economy witnessed a high percentage of unemployment (Zahalka, 1976). The first priority for the Israeli government was to secure employment for the masses of the new Jewish immigrants who came to Israel during the early 1950s and doubled the population of the country within a few years (see Friedlander and Goldscheider, 1979). Therefore, movement of the Arab labor force to the Jewish sector was restricted. Arab laborers were accepted as members of the Histadrut (General Federation of Labor) only in 1959. Before that, they lacked any legitimacy or professional protection. Some interviewees noted that during the early 1950s they were obliged to leave their work because Histadrut's inspectors traced them

----

[1] The classification of plots is derived from the *Report on the Arab Agriculture.* Tel-Aviv University, 1979.

Shefar-A'm: Land Holding

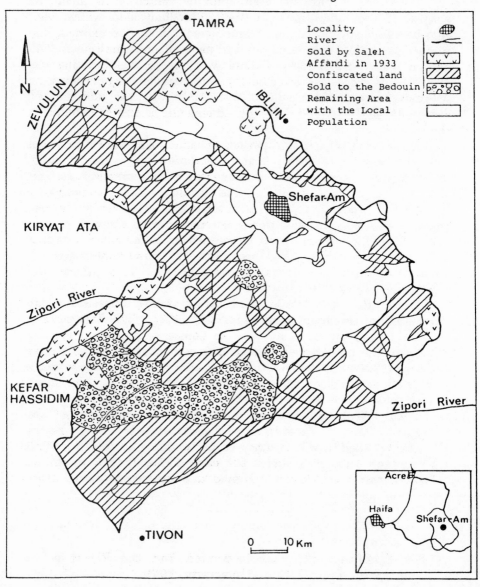

Locality
River
Sold by Saleh Affandi in 1933
Confiscated land
Sold to the Bedouin
Remaining Area with the Local Population

TAMRA

ZEVULUN

IBLLIN

Shefar-Am

KIRYAT ATA

Zipori River

KEFAR HASSIDIM

Zipori River

TIVON

0   10 Km

Acre
Haifa
Shefar-Am

and prevented their work in the Jewish sector.

Analysis of private diaries as well as official documents reflects the several aspects of economic and the occupational situation. One of the unique private documents found in the town provided a profound and a comprehensive picture about the several events which occurred during the first decade after the establishment of Israel. A local teacher used to write a daily review in his diary about the main events, describing the social and economic situation in the town. At the end of each month, he summarized the main events. Analysis of his diaries during the period from 1948 to 1958 revealed the following items: Refugee displacement and settlement in the town, unemployment, rapid increase in the prices and a rise in the black market, fluctuation in the occupational opportunities, improvement in the situation by 1957, and the rapid movement of the labor force to the Jewish sector after 1958. Some typical quotations in these diaries exemplify the main trends.

April 1948: The situation with no change...hostilities (between Arabs and Jews), cessation in all kinds of work; agriculture, trade and industry. Displaced refugees moved to several directions in search of a safe place. Most of them settled in the density areas of the town.

October 1948: The occupational situation from bad to worse. More than 300 youths without any employment, they spend most of their time at the cafe and in the streets.

February 1949: The prices of wheat decreased but the prices of vegetables, oil, and meat increased. Unemployment is observed everywhere, most people are bound to their homes or spend their time in the cafe.

February 1950: God save us!! incredible increase in the prices; kg. soap costs 2 I.L,. and a gallon of oil 18 I.L. Goods disappeared and sold in the black market. Some improvement in occupation was noticed.

July 1951: Continuous uphill in the prices. Stagnancy in occupation.

October 1951: During this month prices increased about 30 percent. Some improvement occurred in occupation.

June 1952: At the beginning of June all the people changed their money. Currency notes with the name Anglo-Palestine were changed by others with the name of Bank Leumi Lisrael.

October 1952: The black market increased drastically. The occupational situation is very difficult and people are complaining about it: those who work in industry, those in trade and those who worked as wage laborers.

February 1953: The cost of life is very high. Shortage in foodstuffs. Unemployment is strongly observed. Most of the people of work age spend their time in the cafe, in the streets and in public places. Stagnancy in commerce because of the shortage of money.

August 1954: There is no change in the occupational situation, uphill in prices and unemployment. Most of the people worked in agriculture.

January 1955: The prices of meat increased sharply, 7.I.L. for kg. The prices of wheat and barley also increased. The drought caused a lot of grievance. The town (Shefar-A'm) still suffers from unemployment.

January 1956: The uphill in prices still observed, shortage in employment for wage laborers excluding in agriculture and quarrying.

January 1957: The prices are still high, but a tangible improvement in occupation has occurred. Some people began to work outside the town.

January 1958: Continuity in the situation concerning prices and occupation. Labor force movement outside the town is observed. Unemployment still observed among strangers (refugees). They move in search of any employment at hand.

It is remarkable that the analysis of the official documents revealed a similar picture to the one reported in these diaries.

Table 2.4 shows that until the late years of the first decade after the establishment of Israel (the transitional period), only 22

TABLE 2.4

LABOR FORCE AGED 15 AND OVER BY BRANCH OF EMPLOYMENT
AND LOCALITY OF WORK IN SHEFAR-A'M, 1981

Branch of Employment	Number	Percent
Locally Employed		
Agriculture and small cattle breeding	383	9.5
Public and financial institutions	215	5.0
Education	245	5.7
Trade and business	490	11.5
Construction	120	2.8
Industry	175	4.1
Employed Outside		
Construction	780	18.2
Industry	638	15.0
Transport and storage	340	8.1
Various private services	–	–
Various automobile services	894	20.1
Total	4280	100.0

percent of the labor force worked outside the locality. The vast majority worked in the locality, mainly in agriculture. Document analysis revealed that among those who worked in agriculture, 50 percent worked their own lands, 28 percent had to work in different jobs in addition to working their lands, and 22 percent were wage laborers. Some continuity in trade and industry was noticed in that period. But in contrast to the pre-1948 period, Shefar-A'm lost its central economic position among the surrounding villages. The restrictions of population movement by the military administration and the destruction of some of the surrounding villages severely affected trade activity, which was localized. This was reflected, among other ways, in the nearly 25 percent decrease in the number of stores and service shops compared with the late years of the Mandatory period.

Documents obtained from the local laborers council indicated that throughout the transitional period 320 laborers, who comprised about one-third of the potential labor force in the town were unemployed or partially employed in temporary jobs. A large part of this reservoir labor force were refugees. The Government allocated a special budget to secure employment for them. Evidence in several municipal documents showed that 1,000 "work days" for the municipality were allocated in 1953 to support employment in local projects for the heads of the refugee households, supervised by the local authority. This situation lasted until the late 1950s. Several municipal documents indicated that until 1957 the municipality requested that the section of Arab Labor Affairs allocate a number of work days in local projects in order to cope with unemployment. In the late 1950s there was a noticeable improvement in the economic situation in the whole country. The demand for Arab labor accelerated (see Israely, 1976). In addition, military administration eased restrictions over Arab movement somewhat. Therefore, by 1959 the reservoir of available local workers moved out of the settlement to become part of the great Arab labor force in search of unskilled work.

In 1961 about 57 percent of the local labor force aged 15 years and over worked outside the locality, mainly in construction and personal and public services. About 43 percent worked within the locality: 24 percent worked in agriculture and 19 percent in trade and business, education, and public service. The dependency of the local labor force on the outside labor market increased from year to year. Changes in the national Israeli economy had immediate repercussions for the town economy. The recession during the Israeli economy in the years 1966 and 1967 strongly affected the occupational situation in the town. Workers in construction were the first to be affected because of the total recession in this branch. The Ministry of Labor allocated special budgets in the framework of "relief works" in order to cope with the problem. Monthly work days were allocated to the adult population (18 years and over) according to social criteria:

12 days for single people
18 days for married people without children
20 days for married people with up to 6 children and
24 days for married people with 6 children and over.

Relief works aimed to support "hand to mouth" income. The maximum work days that a person received throughout the year were restricted to 150 days. Therefore, large segments of the population worked in agriculture or any available work.

The recession ended in 1967. The proletarianization process, which stopped during this period, continued even more rapidly. The labor force working outside the locality accelerated. Within a short period, the local economy lost its significance as a central employer. While Shefar-A'm was deprived of its traditional economic base (agriculture, trade, and crafts), no alternative economic base was created. Even the rise in the standard of living did not free the local labor force from its dependence on outside jobs. On the contrary, dependence increased in proportion to the rise in the standard of living, since the workers worked more or sold plots of land and converted them into other assets in order to reach the coveted standard of living or to preserve their existing standard.

In the 1980s the employment structure of Shefar-A'm does not differ from that typical of other large Arab villages in Israel: local labor is largely dependent on employment in the Jewish center, and the majority are employed in construction and services (private and public), while only 10 percent are employed in agriculture and small cattle breeding. Several factors were responsible for the general drastic decrease in the agricultural labor force among the Arab population after the establishment of Israel, especially after the first decade: the decrease in agricultural land as a result of land confiscations, the increase in the building area, the fragmentation of land as a result of the inheritance system, the mechanization of agriculture, and the asymmetric competition with the Jewish agriculture, where the State investment and subsidy were much larger than in Arab agriculture *(Report on Arab Agriculture 1979:* 3).

All these factors characterize Shefar-A'm as well. However, the decrease in the agricultural lands as a result of the expansion of the building areas may have been more prominent in Shefar-A'm than in other Arab localities because of the high in-migration. The nonagricultural area within the municipal jurisdiction expanded from 3,500 dunam in 1956 to 17,500 dunam in the 1980s. At this time, there are only 8,039 dunam of agricultural land and 1,200 dunam of olive trees, just one-fourth of the agricultural lands under cultivation during the Mandatory period.

An examination of the employment structure in the 1980s among the several groups in the town shows that there is no substantial difference among them (see Table 2.5). About 70 percent of the employees are concentrated in two main economic branches, skilled and unskilled workers. Among them, the overwhelming majority work in the nearby Jewish cities and industrial areas. This trend is part of a wider economic process that has taken place among Arabs in Israel and has resulted in the narrowing of internal class differentiation (see Cohen, 1965; Rosenfeld, 1962). Nevertheless, there remains some residual continuity from the previous group economic structure. Christians are the most likely to work at high status jobs and the least likely to have unskilled jobs. Druze have the highest percentage among the agricultural labor force. In the 1980s Druze own about 60 percent of the agricultural land in Shefar-A'm. The shortage of land among the in-migrant groups, in-migrant Moslems, and Druze El-Jabal is reflected in the total absence of agricultural workers among them.

Analysis of the trade and the service stores shows some residual differences between the several groups. Among 224 stores, 55.3 percent are owned by Christians, 32.2 percent by Moslems, and 12.5 percent by Druze. In-migrant groups owned only about 9 percent of these stores. Excluding the printing press, all other stores serve almost only the local population. As noted earlier, the disappearance of the administrative status and the economic centrality of the town altered the economic dependency between Shefar-A'm and the surrounding villages. The expansion of the metropolitan areas has also contributed to the decrease in the status of the town. There are almost no official services to attract people from other localities. Governmental institutions are concentrated in the nearby cities: Haifa, Nazareth Illit, and Acre.

In sum, Shefar-A'm has witnessed a process of de-urbanization in terms of its economic structure, administrative status, and role as a center for the surrounding villages. This

TABLE 2.5

OCCUPATION OF HEADS OF HOUSEHOLDS AMONG THE SEVERAL GROUPS IN SHEFAR-A'M, 1981

Occupation	Local Moslems	In-migrant Moslems	Christians	Local Druze	Druze El-Jabal	Total
Academic, professional	7.3	6.5	12.7	5.9	2.3	7.0
Clerical and related workers	3.8	2.5	4.2	3.9	5.6	4.0
Administrators and managers	3.0	4.5	4.5	1.9	2.0	4.5
Financing and business services	4.0	2.8	5.8	2.3	1.5	3.8
Skilled workers in industry building transport and other skilled workers	49.6	48.0	51.0	37.0	38.0	48.5
Unskilled workers	23.3	35.7	17.3	27.0	50.6	24.2
Agricultural workers	9.0	0.0	4.5	22.0	0.0	8.0
Total	100.0	100.0	100.0	100.0	100.0	100.0
N	403	373	706	225	28	1765

process started during the late years of the Mandatory Period (in the late 1940s), but accelerated in particular after the establishment of Israel. As a result the internal economic dependency among the several groups within the locality and between Shefar-A'm and the surrounding villages was replaced by an overall dependency of all these groups on the external dominant Jewish sector.

Group Status Structure

Shefar-A'm's previous position as an industrial, economic, and administrative center attracted population movement to the town throughout several periods. This reinforced its pluralistic structure: Moslems, Christians, and Druze came during the pre-1948 period, and later in-migrant groups included refugees, Bedouins, and Druze El-Jabal. Analysis of the group status structure in the town reveals that group affiliation is not only a social indicator, but to a political and economic indicator as well. The struggle for the control of the local power system has been carried out at the group level, while the individual and the family were submerged. Moreover, the extent of social security at the individual and the family levels has been affected for a long time by group affiliation.

Our analysis of the group status structure will be placed in the framework of a multi-dimensional approach to minority-majority status. The main dimensions of groups status are: political hegemony, regional status and external aid, minority feeling, demographic size, and economic dominance. The first three dimensions will be examined in detail. The last two will be included within the others, since they were discussed in detail earlier (see Al-Haj, 1985).

Political Hegemony

As noted earlier, Shefar-A'm was one of the first settlements in the north to be granted city rights and to be administered by an elected city council. Control of the local administration became the touchstone for determining power balance between the various local religious groups. The first city council was appointed in 1910 by the regional governor (the Ottoman "mūdir"); it was composed of five Christians (one of whom was the mayor) and one Druze. No Moslem member was appointed. This composition clearly

48

demonstrated the great differentiation in the economic position of the various communities--membership in the city council was the exclusive right of landowners and tax-payers, both during the Ottoman period and, later, under the British mandate (Maoz, 1962:233).

In the wake of the 1948 war, the city council of Shefar-A'm ceased to function. For the next three years, the mayor dealt with the affairs of the town from his home. In 1951 a new city council, consisting of seven members in addition to the mayor, was appointed; it was composed of three Christians, three Druze, and two Moslems.

The composition of the council was in a way a continuation of the situation from the pre-1948 period, with representation along communal lines. The Christians retained their dominance and continued to hold the post of mayor. The strengthening of the Druze's position after the formation of Israel was immediately reflected in their representation on the council. For the first time in Shefar-A'm's history, this community was represented by three members, almost one-third of the council's membership, although the community itself accounted for only 20 percent of the population. The Moslems remained in their marginal position, and their two representatives on the council had no influence whatsoever on the municipal procedures.

The economic and sociodemographic changes which occurred during the first decade after the establishment of Israel drastically influenced the power struggle between the religious groups and the kinship groups (hamulas) during the second decade. Following the birth of the State of Israel, and in particular after the first decade, when Shefar-A'm became economically dependent upon the external resources in the Jewish sector, internal economic inter-dependence lost its significance. As a result, the conflicts became aggravated and groups which had hitherto been at the periphery began moving towards the center and participating in the struggle for political control. This development was reflected in the dynamics of change in the inter-religious power balance. More particularly, the Moslems, who had been at the periphery because of their economic dependence on the Christians and the Druze, at first showed no inclination to participate in the struggle for political control. It was only in the middle 1960s, after the economic foundations of the systems of social status had crumbled, that the Moslems began to reveal signs of communal consolidation in their struggle for the mayorality, and towards the end of that decade they reached their goal. This became possible also due to the fact that Moslems, for the first time of the town's history, attained population equality with Christians (roughly 40 percent for each group).

Regional Status and External Aid

On March 31, 1947 there were 1,253,000 Arabs in Palestine, of whom 1,091,000 were Moslems (86.3 percent), 146,000 Christians (11.7 percent), and 16,000 Druze and others (2 percent) (Government of Palestine, 1947). From these figures it is clear that the Moslems constituted the overwhelming majority, a fact reflected in their control of national economic resources and of their presence as the political and social elite among Palestinian Arabs. This was also the situation in the Shefar-A'm region, and this regional pattern deeply affected communal relations in the town.

The weakness of the overall central government in the period before the establishment of the State of Israel caused the individual citizen to feel insecure and to live in permanent fear for his life, family, and property. He was therefore compelled to seek security through affiliation with a group which was as large as possible and in which the binding elements were stronger than the dividing ones (e.g., clan, neighborhood, sect, community). Such groups were not only reinforced from within, but also from without, in particular by groups or settlements with whom they had close ties, preferably based upon blood ties or common descent. These external relations, and their potential or actual aid in case of need, were extremely important for members of every community.

The network of relationships among religious group members in Shefar-A'm was very wide. In many cases these links were of an individual kind and found expression in such areas as trade work, reciprocal visits, participation in various social events, and so forth. However, in addition to these kinds of ties, each group had its own special external orientation of a communal nature.

The Moslems chiefly maintained relations with the surrounding villages that had an outspoken Moslem majority. Among the 22 villages which constituted the Shefar-A'm district, 18 were Moslem villages and four had a mixed Moslem-Christian population. There were no Druze villages in the district. The Moslem community of Shefar-A'm therefore enjoyed the position of a community belonging to the regional majority, a status which positively affected their relations with others since they could count on immediate help from the surrounding villages in case of a blood feud or other conflicts. Groups from outside the settlement frequently interfered in individual disputes and even exploited the chaos created by divisions in order to steal or to extort, sometimes against the wish of the local Moslems.

The Druze maintained strong ties with the villages in the Golan Heights, Lebanon, and Jabal El-Arab in Syria. In the diaries of one of the Druze Sheikhs, we found reports of frequent reciprocal visits between the Druze in Shefar-A'm and their co-religionists in these villages. We also found an extensive correspondence between them. The Druze in Lebanon and Syria maintained a deep interest in the vicissitudes of their brethren in Shefar-A'm. For example, in 1937 one of the Druze notables from Jabal El-Arab sent a letter to the manager of the Arab Bank in Haifa requesting him to intervene personally with the Moslems in Shefar-A'm in order to improve their relations with their Druze neighbors. Among other things he wrote:

> "...we know that the affair started as an incident between two people, and that fate hit one of them: the government arrested the suspect and he will be brought to trial. The question is whether it was just that the surrounding villages attacked the Druze, committed acts of destruction, frightened women and children, and offended the men's honor. The same thing could have happened when Ṣaleh Affendi was killed, and were it not for the mercy of God, who revealed the real murderer, acts of violence would have been committed of which none would know the end. Brothers in Jabal El-Arab know what happened and in the name of our brotherhood in religion, language, and country, we try to do all in our might to ensure the peace of the Druze in Shefar-A'm and to preserve the good relations between you and your brethren, the Druze of Jabal El-Arab and of Mount Lebanon who have spared no effort to support every Arab cause and in particular the Palestinian cause, I beg to remark that you shall shortly receive similar letters from Sulṭan Bāsha al-Atrash and other Druze notables..."

In the rioting between Druze and Moslems in 1939, the Druze of Jabal El-Arab also intervened. We found a report dated January 31, 1939 about a Druze delegation from Jabal El-Arab which had come especially to reach a compromise between the communities and to restore peace.

Although this external aid was important for the local Druze community, it nonetheless was not sufficient to ensure their safety. This was because of the geographical distance, and because the Druze from these outside areas did not intervene physically, but instead played the part of mediator between the two "Moslem branches", a reference to the fact that they regarded the Druze and Moslems as two branches of the same religion.

For their part, the Christians of Shefar-A'm maintained an urban orientation in their relations with the outside world. Their principal ties were with the urban Christian communities of Haifa, Acre, Jaffa, and even Beirut. These relations became closer in the course of time and led to the migration of Christian families from Shefar-A'm to these places. Some informants reported that well-to-do Christians used to spend most of their time in Beirut. These relations, however, were not translated into actual assistance to the Christians in Shefar-A'm and had little influence on their relations with the other communities. It may be assumed that during the Mandatory Period there was no need for such assistance since the political and social elite of the town consisted mainly of Christian notables whose close relations with the British authorities bolstered their position both within and outside the settlement.

The formal aid the local communities, and in particular the Moslems, had received from their co-religionists prior to the formation of Israel lost much of its practical significance after 1948. Following the 1948 war only 160,000 of the 700,000 Arabs who had lived in the territory which became Israel remained in the country. Of these, 68.7 percent were Moslems, 21.2 percent Christians, and 9.1 percent Druze (Amram, 1965). Since the establishment of Israel, the Arab population has expanded at a fast rate, primarily because of their high birth rate and not as the result of immigration. The proportional division of the communities has not changed much, although the Moslem population has slightly increased in relation to the other communities since their birth rate has been higher.

Immediately after 1948, relations with Arab countries were cut off, the borders were closed, and the links between the Israeli Arab population and their co-religionists beyond the "green line" were cut off. Relationships outside their own settlement but within the borders were also drastically reduced. Many of the surrounding settlements, with which fruitful relations had existed in the past, were destroyed: of the 22 villages in the Shefar-A'm region, eight were destroyed. Six of these were Moslem villages and two had a mixed Moslem-Christian population. Moreover, a military government was installed in areas with a large Arab population, including the Western Galilee where Shefar-A'm was located. The military government (which continued until 1966) restricted the movement of the local population who had to obtain a special permit for entering or leaving the region for a limited period of time.

An additional reason for the changing social relations with other Arab settlements was the weakening of economic interdependence. As was pointed out earlier, the transformation of the employment structure in the Arab sector led to the same pattern in all the Arab settlements: almost total dependence on wage labor in the Jewish centers, and the simultaneous reduction or elimination of the economic interdependence of the Arab settlements. This development deeply affected the social relations between these settlements and reduced the possibilities of mutual influence. In addition to these factors, the restraining element of a strong central government which imposed law and order must also be added. The development of the judicial system and the presence of the police was felt in every settlement. This greatly reduced the possibility of spontaneous action such as vengeance and the exploitation of individual conflicts to stir up inter-communal tension.

Partly as a result of the loss of these informal regional supports, the Israeli government's formal powers became the decisive element in issues of economy and politics. One of the striking features of the Israeli government's policy toward the Arab minority was its attempt to turn the Arabs into a "mixture of minorities" with the goal of splitting the population into a great number of tiny minorities (Smooha, 1980:17). For example, the Druze were granted the status of a separate community, and in 1957 the Minister of Religious Affairs issued regulations which recognized the Druze as a religious community. Four years later, in October 1961, the religious leadership of the Druze was recognized as a "Religious Council" headed by Sheikh Amin Ţarif, while in 1962 the Knesset completed the process by approving the Law on Druze Religious Courts (Falah, 1974; Stendel, 1972). The most important move in this regard was the application of the Law on Compulsory Army Service to the Druze in 1956--since that time Druze males have been conscripted into the Israeli Army. The fostering of the Druze community as a separate religious and political entity found further expression in the change of the "nationality paragraph" in their identify card from "Arab" to "Druze" and, finally, in the recognition of separate Druze education and the establishment of a Druze Education Committee in 1976.

The Bedouin also received special treatment in the attempt to turn them into a separate community. This policy was expressed in several ways, the most recent being Prime Minister Shamir's separate meetings with representatives of the Arabs and the Bedouin during a series of meetings with the minorities in Israel *(The Jerusalem Post,* January 10, 1984).

A similar attempt was made to emphasize the special character of the Christian community. A recommendation outlining this policy may be found in a Labour Party document: "A special status should be given to the Christian communities and their special character should be stressed in order to distinguish them from the Moslem majority, so as to prevent Arab organization on a national level in which Moslem, nationalistic tendencies often dictate the forms of action" (Smooha, 1980:17).

These differentiating tendencies have also been apparent in the attitude of the government towards the various communities in Shefar-A'm. For a variety of political and ecological reasons, the Druze minority has received particular political support in Israel. Since the first days of Israeli statehood, the leadership of the Druze community has become increasingly powerful and it has strengthened its influence over the other local communities. One of the main Druze leaders, Sheikh Ṣaleh Khneifis, was a Knesset Member until 1959, and he is still regarded as one of the outstanding personalities in the region. During the 1950s he was the link between the government and the populations of Shefar-A'm and the neighboring villages. Many individual as well as clan interests could be furthered through his mediation, which was especially important when the local population was ruled by the military government.

The Druze have also held a pivotal position in the Shefar-A'm city council and have participated in each coalition. Consequently, the Druze community has become the central factor in the shaping of the internal politics and the division of power and economic resources. It should be added, however, that the religious and political particularism of the Druze is less conspicuous in Shefar-A'm than in the villages with a homogenous Druze population. The fact that the Druze in Shefar-A'm reside in a mixed town, side by side with two other groups who constitute an overwhelming majority, has prevented them from becoming entirely absorbed by the trend towards Druze particularism which has generally characterized the Druze community in Israel (Druze children in Shefar-A'm attend local Arab schools which are not supervised by the Druze Educational Committee).

The development towards particularism of the Moslem

Bedouin is less striking, but it too merits attention. Many Bedouin families were settled in Shefar-A'm in the framework of the program for Bedouin population concentrations. A few young Bedouin serve in the Israeli Army on a voluntary basis. Some Bedouin affairs are dealt with by the Commission for Bedouin Affairs which was established by the Prime Minister's Advisor for Arab Affairs, but there is as yet no deep separatism. Christian particularism has been unsuccessful on the local and the national level alike. Although some signs in this direction can currently be seen, there is no indication that the tendency is developing.

Minority Feelings

The feelings of being a member of a minority group are subjective and it is therefore difficult to determine their dimensions and scope. This becomes even more difficult when we try to analyze a system of relations in the past, even if it is not a remote past. Moreover, when one attempts to understand these past feelings through interviews with people who lived during a previous time period, the risk is great of judging the past by the standards of the present and being prejudiced by changes that have occurred since then. In order to remain consistent in our analysis of the two periods--before and after the establishment of Israel, we shall try to understand the minority feelings of the several religious communities by interpreting behavioral elements reflected in various events, and by analyzing the regional and social composition of the settlement.

In the pre-state period minority feelings were especially strong among the Druze. They were physically threatened by the Moslems who were then the most powerful group in the region. This threat became real when, for example, a number of Moslem families without land seized Druze lands and arrogated to themselves the right to cultivate them, all the time ignoring the protests of the original owners. The Druze victims were unable to regain their land, and according to some informants they were afraid to submit a complaint to the authorities. They appealed therefore for help to Şaleh Affendi, a rich Moslem from Kafr Makir, who was a powerful and influential man among the Moslems of the region.

The Druze initially sought unofficial guarantees for their safety. They tried, for example, to recruit the support of leading personalities who held positions of power. But when such guarantees could not be obtained, they began to look for an alternative and turned to the official authorities, such as the British Mandatory government. Yet their contacts with the government merely aggravated their conflict with the Moslems, and this in turn led to the enforcement of their particularistic tendency and to a closing of the ranks. In the diary of a member of the Druze community, we read that "...in the night of 13 August 1939 the rebels attacked the Druze in Shefar-A'm because they refused to cooperate with them. Three Druze were killed, and the relations with the Moslems deteriorated even further when several houses belonging to Moslems were destroyed by the British authorities in the wake of a complaint by the Druze about the incident."

The Arab revolt of 1939 and the ensuing danger for the Druze, who were harassed by the rebels, greatly intensified their minority feelings. The revolt was thus a turning point for their Druze in the development and consolidation of a particularistic Druze identity in Palestine and, consequently, in their rapprochement with the Israeli establishment. This development can be clearly traced in several Druze settlements. During March 1939, for example, 65 Druze leaders from Osofya sent a letter to the British commander in Haifa, in which they wrote: "We, the notables and elders of Osofya, herewith express our deep gratitude to the Mandatory government which has done much to preserve the safety in the village by handing over 19 rifles to the local guards. Since these rifles were delivered we feel that order has been restored, and the rebels no longer dare to enter the settlement..."

A further example of the Druze minority feelings is provided by an analysis of those composition of the areas continuing a Druze population. As mentioned above, the Druze were among the first to settle in the new areas of Shefar-A'm. They founded two important neighborhoods--one in the settlement's nucleus, and the second to the east of it. When in the eighteenth century Moslem families settled in Shefar-A'm, the eastern neighborhood became a mixed Druze-Moslem district as some of these families settled around the existing Druze. The fact that the Druze lived in a mixed neighborhood doubtless enhanced their minority feelings and their feeling of being permanently threatened. Consequently, when tempers became heated in the 1939 riots and the Druze felt that their lives and families were in danger, they left their houses and moved to the fringes of the homogeneous Druze district in the town's nucleus. The Druze residential neighborhoods have since become increasingly homogeneous religiously.

Minority feelings were expressed occasionally by the

56

Christians as well, though to a much lesser degree than the Druze. They constituted the political and social elite of the settlement, and their position was strengthened by their relations with the British authorities. The one-sided economic dependence on them by the local Moslem population also enhanced their feelings of social security.

The Moslems of Shefar-A'm, on the other hand, had majority feelings in the past because of their strong position in the region and the support they could count on from the Moslems in the nearby villages. These majority feelings could be observed in many behavioral patterns, of which we have mentioned a few in our description of the violence between Moslems and members of other communities. Nevertheless, this majority feeling was not sufficient to foster their majority status, since they were a marginal group in terms of their economic status and were the last settlers in the town.

As to the minority feelings following the establishment of Israel, we must distinguish between the local, internal level and the national, external level. With the proclamation of Israeli independence, the concept of "minority status" assumed an entirely different meaning since all of the Arab communities suddenly belonged to the non-Jewish minority.

The Israeli-Arab conflict and the recurring wars turned the Israeli Arabs into a "hostile minority" (Smooha, 1976). The economic, social, and political changes which the Arab population experienced, and the special relations of Jews and Arabs in Israel, enhanced the latter's minority status in the national sphere. The various Arab communities and groups in Shefar-A'm, like elsewhere in Israel, strongly felt that they belonged to the non-Jewish minority. During the first decade of Israeli statehood, these minority feelings on the local level were especially pronounced for the Moslem community of Shefar-A'm. Many Moslem families became separated, and some left for Arab countries, especially Lebanon. Those who later returned from Lebanon and decided to remain in Shefar-A'm lived with the persistent fear that they would not be granted Israeli citizenship because they had left the settlement during the war and were regarded as "absentees". The Moslem community lost its sense of being a regional majority which it had fostered for hundreds of years, and became instead part of the Arab minority in Israel. Moreover, the Moslems were not part of the government's particularistic approach. Therefore, they did not enjoy the sense of security which government support might have given them. The influx of internal refugees, almost all of them Moslems, intensified the feeling of having a "minority status", for these refugees were a group of broken have-nots.

In the course of time the Moslems began to derive inner strength from the growing number of in-migrant Moslems and from the settlement's changing social structure due to the large-scale economic changes. These, changes, in turn, led to a radical change in the social status structure which made it possible for the Moslems to control positions of local power.

Minority feelings were also felt by the in-migrant Moslems, the Bedouin and the internal refugees, all of whom had the status of a "gharib" (stranger). They had come to the town empty-handed and were forced to compete for the existing resources which were in the hands of the local population. Members of these groups developed a strong feeling of belonging to a minority which, on the one hand, wished to defend itself, but on the other, wanted to become integrated into the majority. These feelings were clearly reflected in their housing patterns and the composition of their neighborhoods. They lived close to one another in crowded buildings, and eventually created sub-districts within the heterogeneous districts of the town. In our interviews with many of these in-migrants, their minority feelings could easily be distinguished, and it was also clear that these feelings led them to demonstrate their strength in various ways, in particular by voting during municipal elections.

Differences in the social status between in-migrant groups and locals have decreased in the second generation. The demographic and the socioeconomic changes noted before contributed to the integration into the community of the second generation from a position of strength and not from a point of weakness. This is reflected, among other ways, in the patterns of intermarriages. For example, in the 1950s there were no marriage relations between local Moslems and in-migrant Moslems, while in the 1980s this type of marriage constituted about 30 percent of the marriages among in-migrant Moslems. In addition, during the last decade, a noticeable movement of young in-migrant spouses occurred from their homogeneous neighborhoods to the mixed neighborhoods in the local area. However, despite the integration of the migratory groups, their minority status has not changed completely. Asymmetric relations between them and the locals still exist in several ways. Therefore, they may be viewed as transitional rather than assimilated.

The minority feelings among the Christians after 1948 were much weaker than those of the Moslems, since they had always been a minority. Their minority status did not make them feel weak; they continued to be the dominant economic and political group in the town until the late 1960s when, as we have seen, the Moslems again became the major community. Even when they lost their political power, it took the Christians many years to resign themselves to the new balance of power. However, even though the Christians lost their political hegemony and economic dominance, they did not become a marginal group.

The changes experienced by the Druze are of special interest. This religious group passed, in a very short period of time, from a persecuted minority to one with feelings of strength. The process of religious particularization which had already begun in the pre-state days was accelerated and consolidated after the rise of the state. Dozens of young Druze volunteered for the Israeli Army, particularly for the border police units. In 1956 the compulsory army draft was applied to the young Druze of Shefar-A'm with the approval and encouragement of the community's elders (Stendel, 1972).

The feelings of strength among the Druze are also reflected in the reversal of the process of outside assistance. Before 1948 the local Druze needed the help of their brethren from Jabal El-Arab in Syria and Mount Lebanon; more recently the Druze have closed ranks to help their co-religionists beyond the borders. This was demonstrated for example, by their solidarity with the Druze in the Golan Heights when the government imposed a curfew on the Druze villages because of their refusal to accept Israeli Law.

During the recent Lebanese War, the Druze openly sided with their community in the Shuf Mountains and tried to help them in various ways, such as requesting permission to volunteer for their militia, collecting money, and organizing as a political pressure group within Israel. The Druze of Shefar-A'm actively participated in these developments. They organized a meeting in the "Khilwi", the Druze house of prayer, during August 1983 at which the speakers stressed that Israel had a commitment towards the Druze in Lebanon because of the contribution of the Israeli Druze to the state.

> The Druze in Israel are the most loyal allies of the State of Israel. They have sacrificed the best of their sons who participated in the wars of Israel, as is witnessed by the 290 Druze soldiers who have fallen since the birth of the State. This is a large number in relation to the number of Druze in Israel, which does not exceed 50,000. Our morale is evidently very high, we have done the

government great favors and we don't think that they will deny this. (El Anbǎ, 7 August 1983)

These feelings of strength or feelings of security, are also reflected in new patterns of residence. The Druze passed from the agglomerate model to the "dispersed residential area" model. Today, many Druze houses can be seen scattered far from the densely populated areas of town, which has served as an incentive for the municipal council to expand its jurisdiction and, consequently, the town's building zone.

Nevertheless, even in the Druze community a group exists that expresses minority feelings. This is the Druze El-Jabal who compose a small minority. Their relations with the other groups of the Druze community are formal, and there is almost no intermarriage between them. Since the state's proclamation only two young men from Druze El-Jabal have married local Druze girls. They maintain relations mainly with members of their own group in Dāliat el-Karmel and Osofya. One of the Druze El-Jabal interviewees expressed himself sharply:

> We feel as if we are a minority within a minority. We feel that we are an alienated minority within the Druze community which itself is part of the Arab minority in Israel. The local Druze still regard us as refugees and every achievement by one of our group arouses their envy and hatred. I feel more at home, in speech, visits, and recreation, with the Druze El-Jabal families in Osofya and Daliat el-Karmel than with the local Druze.

In sum, examination of the several elements which comprise the minority-majority status reveals that each religious group has a mixture of minority-majority elements in its status structure. After the establishment of Israel, in particular after the second decade, a transitional status emerged between the minority-majority status. It was reflected in the status of Moslems and the second generation of the in-migrant groups.

In the aggregate, during the pre-1948 period, Christians clearly had a majority status. Moslems and Druze had a minority status, which was, however, felt more strongly by the Druze. This situation continued somewhat during the first decade after the establishment of Israel. But it differed in the sense that Druze passed to a position of perceived strength, while Moslems retained a deep feeling of minority status. The economic and sociodemographic changes which occurred during the first decade found their expression in the late 1960s, when Moslems became the dominant political group along with their coalition with Druze. Moslems have not fully established their majority status because the period since their status replacement has been relatively short and because the change in their status has not been reinforced by internal patterns of economic dependency. Therefore, they may be viewed as a transitional, rather than a majority, group.

The in-migrant groups have had a minority status relative to locals since the very beginning. Some change has occurred in the status of the second generation, who have become more integrated. Nevertheless, they are still not fully integrated. They also may be viewed as transitional rather than assimilated.

What is the impact of these contextual factors of the community on family lifestyles and family processes? How do these factors combine with the individual factors to affect family patterns? What is the nature of the relationship between the dynamics of the group status structure and the changes in the several familial units? These questions will be addressed in detail in the following chapters.

3

The Kinship Structure

Kinship structure is considered a central familial structure in many societies. Its importance lies in the fact that it can serve as a framework of allocation for goods, services, power, social interaction, and self identification (see Levy, 1965). The definition of kinship structure is controversial and depends on whether one views the kinship structure in substantive terms, functional terms, or a mixture of both (see Schneider, 1965). Levy (1965:2) has defined kinship structure as "that portion of the analytic and concrete structures of a society in terms of which, in addition to other orientations sometimes equally if not even more important, the membership of the units and the nature of the solidarity among the members of the units was determined by orientation to the fact of biological relatedness and/or sexual intercourse." This definition is problematic since it emphasizes the biological relatedness, rather than the functional or the social relatedness. The fact of biological relatedness is difficult to establish in most cases (Schneider, 1965:91). In addition, the emphasis of biological relatedness may ignore the social significance of the kinship structure as a unit which aims to fulfill some basic needs for individuals and groups (see Pelzel, 1970).

Studies conducted in Middle Eastern societies have shown that the definition of the kinship structure in terms of biological relatedness is incomplete. Actually, links with the kinship group may be social and not necessarily biological. A study conducted on Kufr al-Ma, a Jordanian village, noted that "improvisation of genealogical links and claims of descent group membership were regarded as the traditional procedure for legitimizing village residence" (Antoun, 1972:110). Another study conducted on two

63

suburbs in Beriut noted that the kinship structure might expand or shrink depending on the ambition and power of its leaders. "It is not exactly true to say that large families tend to produce prominent men: on the contrary, prominent men tend to produce large families" (Khuri, 1976:96). The significance of the kinship structure, therefore, lies in its flexibility in allowing individuals or segments to shift descent from one line to another without losing identity (Khuri, 1976).

In our analysis of the kinship group (hamula), we adopted the definition which takes into consideration both the biological and the social relatedness. We define the hamula or the patrilineage as a patrilineal descent group composed of all the members related biologically to the common great-grandfather, or members who have related themselves socially to a certain hamula by fictive relatedness in order to obtain the advantage of the hamula protection and rights along with the hamula responsibilities and commitments (see Rosenfeld, 1973).

The hamula is a central familial unit in Arab Middle Eastern society. Blood bonds are stronger than any other bonds and require deep commitment and responsibility (see Patai, 1983; Abu-Gosh, 1972; Lutfiyya, 1970). Most importantly, the kinship affiliation grants legitimacy to the individual's position in the local community. Involvement in the community can be achieved only through the descent group (see Antoun, 1972). Three main role provided by the hamula are the political, the social, and the economic roles (see Rosenfeld, 1972, 1964; Khuri, 1975). The political role is reflected in the protection that the hamula gives for its members and their property and its functioning as a political framework in the struggle over the local power system. The social role is reflected mainly in the hamula's functioning as a central unit in the marriage market and as a network for permanent social interaction. The economic role is reflected in the hamula's functioning as a source of economic aid (see Al-Haj, 1979; Ginat, 1975; Rosenfeld, 1964).

The question may be raised: what is the nature of the current status of the kinship structure among Arabs in Israel? The answer provided by the modernization approach is that the kinship structure would be drastically undermined. The occupational transformation, the rapid increase in education, the exposure to mass media and other modern institutions, and the intensive contact with the Jewish population as agents of westernization would tend to reinforce the modern systems and diminish and break down the traditional kinship system. This process includes several elements as noted in chapter 1. First, the modernization

64

process is an all encompassing process. The social, political, and economic roles of the hamula, then, would be affected in the same way and in the same direction, i.e., they would decrease drastically. Second, since the modernization process is continuous, the decline of the hamula roles would be continuous. A cessation of kinship change or reversal toward greater kinship reinforcement would not be expected. Third, there is a high correlation between developing modern attitudes and becoming modern in behavior (Inkeles and Smith, 1974; Armer and Youtz, 1971). Hence, changes in the normative base of the hamula would accompany changes in actual behavior.

Studies conducted among Arabs in Israel have reached several conclusions regarding the effect of the modernization process on the Arab kinship structure. Some have noted that the modernization and the penetration of the democratic system to the local elections weakened the hamula system and reinforced the trend towards social convergence with the Jewish sector (see Avitsour, 1978). Others reached the opposite conclusions, that the several changes which occurred after the establishment of Israel not only did not weaken the hamula, but contributed to its reinforcement (see Cohen, 1965; Rosenfeld, 1972; Nakhleh, 1975). The later trend was viewed by some researchers as a transitional phase, since modernization forces and democratic elections are expected to ultimately weaken the hamula organization (see Layish, 1975).

The weakness of these arguments lies in the fact that most of them take for granted that the Arab kinship structure was strong before the establishment of Israel. This is because they are solely based on a current examination of the hamula status, while treatment of the previous situation is made by inference. Few of these studies were based on retrospective data (see Rosenfeld, 1972). The basic assumption is that Arab society maintained strong kinship structure as an integral part of its traditional structure before the establishment of Israel. However, Cohen (1965) has noted that this assumption is misleading since the kinship structure was weakened drastically in the last years of the Mandatory Period after the abolishment of the musha system (the communal land) and the development of Arab national organizations. Another weakness of these studies is that no clear distinction is made between the behavioral level and the normative level. Most scholars have merged the two levels together. These approaches are based on the assumption that actual behavior is synonymous with norms (see Avitsour, 1978; Kressel, 1976; Datan, 1972).

In this chapter we will examine the hamula's social role as reflected in the patrilineal endogamy system (marriage within the hamula), its political role as reflected in the local elections, and its economic role as reflected in the mutual economic aid between hamula members. The changes in the hamula status will be traced throughout three periods: the last years of the Ottoman Period, the Mandatory Period, and after the establishment of Israel. The longitudinal analysis will provide the basis for a better understanding of the present status of the kinship structure and the nature of the changes which occurred throughout the several periods. Our major questions are: What are the main changes which occurred in the kinship structure from the period before the establishment of Israel compared to the period after the State was established? What is the effect of the modernization process on the kinship structure? Is the effect of modernization uniform for both normative and behavioral levels? What is the relative effect of the modernization factors on kinship patterns compared with the effects of economic and the sociodemographic factors?

Marriage Patterns and the Hamula

Patrilineal endogamy has been noted by some scholars as the distinctive aspect of the Middle Eastern Society (see Caldwell, 1977; Patai, 1970). Several attempts have been made to explain this phenomenon. Despite the wide range and diversity of these explanations, they may be classified into two main groups: pragmatic explanations and cultural ideological explanations. Studies affiliated with the first group view patrilineal endogamy as a practical answer for demographic, economic, ecological, and political needs and constraints (see Fernea and Malarky, 1975; Granquist, 1935; Rosenfeld, 1972). Studies affiliated with the second group tend to view endogamy as an ideal system deeply embedded in Arab culture (see Kressel, 1976; Patai, 1970; Caldwell, 1977). The first group tends to see endogamy as a dynamic and changeable phenomenon, affected by alterations in the social, economic, or political system under which it was created. The second group tends to see the phenomenon as stagnant and changeless, since the ideal system and cultural values are retained by the transference from one generation to another. The examination of patrilineal endogamy in Shefar-A'm has shown that this phenomenon is dynamic and is deeply affected by

66

the sociodemographic, political, and economic changes in the community. Our analysis has indicated that the hamula is currently the major social unit in the marriage market. Druze are the most endogamous religious group; among them 50 percent of the marriages are patrilineal, compared with 38 percent among local Moslems, 21 percent among Christians, and 20 percent among refugee Moslems. Similar findings were indicated by a survey conducted later on the Arab rural population in the western Galilee region in Israel (Freundlich and Hino, 1984). The observed percentages of endogamy in this survey were: 49 percent among Druze, 40 percent among Moslems, and 29 percent among Christians.

There are two ways to examine whether current proportions of patrilineal endogamy have changed over time. Comparisons can be made with research conducted in other Arab localities in Israel and diachronic comparison can be made within the same locality. Considering the modernization which has already taken place among the Arab population in Israel, patrilineal endogamy is expected to have decreased markedly as a result of the weakening of the traditional social units based on descent lines, blood kin, or affinal relations (see Avitsour, 1978). However, empirical comparisons with other communities and over time do not support this conclusion. Based on extensive research conducted on a mixed Moslem-Christian village in the Galilee, Rosenfeld concluded that there was a noticeable stability, and even increase, in the proportion of patrilineal endogamy for several periods (Rosenfeld, 1972). Other research, conducted on a Moslem village during the 1950s and 1970s, came to similar conclusions. During the first period, the proportion of marriages within the hamula was 50 percent, compared with 52.6 percent in the second period (see Cohen, 1965; Habash, 1977).

Similar findings were derived from our longitudinal survey (covering the period 1931-81) of 2,586 marriages, based on reports of clergy who conducted marriage ceremonies among the several groups in Shefar-A'm. Several conclusions can be drawn from the data (see table 3.1):

(1) Comparison between the Mandatory period and the first decade after the establishment of the State of Israel indicates a trend of continuity in patrilineal endogamy, with some decrease among Moslems.

(2) The second decade after the establishment of Israel was characterized by the highest level of patrilineage

67

TABLE 3.1

TRENDS IN PATRILINEAL ENDOGAMY AMONG MAIN GROUPS IN
SHEFAR-A'M, 1931-81

Groups Type of Marriage-Period	Moslems Local	Refugees	Christians Local	Druze Local
1931-47				
Same patrilineage	34.0	–	21.0	26.0
Same locality, different patrilineage	41.0	–	64.0	64.0
Different locality, different patrilineage	25.0	–	15.0	10.0
1949-58				
Same patrilineage	28.0	16.0	23.0	32.0
Same locality, different patrilineage	67.0	59.0	72.0	62.0
Different locality, different patrilineage	5.0	25.0	5.0	6.0
1959-69				
Same patrilineage	40.0	24.0	24.0	51.0
Same locality, different patrilineage	50.0	64.0	68.0	43.0
Different locality, different patrilineage	10.0	12.0	8.0	6.0
1970-81				
Same patrilineage	36.0	20.0	21.0	50.0
Same locality, different patrilineage	58.0	68.0	69.0	40.0
Different locality, different patrilineage	6.0	12.0	10.0	10.0
Number of cases (2586)	922	274	1026	364

marriage among the several groups.

(3) Comparison between the two last decades indicates stability with a little decrease.

(4) Comparison between the two main periods, before and after the establishment of Israel, shows the proportion of patrilineal marriages has conspicuously increased.

More significant are the differential religious changes which occurred. During the Mandatory Period, extra-local marriages constituted a significant proportion of Moslem marriages (one-fourth of the total marriages). During the first decade of the state, extra-local marriages were reduced significantly among the three religious groups, with Moslems experiencing the greatest reduction. However, internal refugees had the highest proportion of this type of marriage during the same period.

Paradoxically, the pattern of patrilineal marriage implies the continuation of traditionalism. This, despite the expectation that the local community, having achieved a more advanced stage of modernization, would not return to more traditionalism (see Inkeles and Smith, 1974). This leads to the question: Is marriage a system based on the influence of the hamula and other kinship structures, or is it based on individual decision making?

The data indicate that current patrilineal marriages are not the outcome of hamula alliances, despite the hamula's strong political status. Most of these marriages are the outcome of individual decision making. Only 10 percent of the males and 15 percent of the females who had been married within the hamula reported that their marriage was a result of the hamula or the extended family decision. In contrast, 70 percent of the males and 52 percent of the females reported that it was the result of their personal decision making. The rest reported that it was a mixed personal-hamula decision. If the decision making is mainly personal, why has the hamula remained the main unit in the marriage market? Why did socioeconomic modernization not result in the modernization of the hamula? To address these questions, we need to examine the marriage market and the field of eligibles.

Three main parallel processes took place in the marriage market after the establishment of Israel. First, the previous marriage market, in which the hamula was only one potential resource along with other major resources, became fractionated. Second, as a result of several sociodemographic factors, the hamula and the new kinship group among the refugees became important political and social units. Consequently, they functioned as major units in the recreated marriage market. Third, the effectiveness of these units was intensified as a parallel process of group concentration. Let us examine each of these processes in detail.

The sociodemographic changes which occurred after the establishment of Israel resulted in a drastic decrease in the marriage market, which became localized among the Arab population as well as the local community. The process of localization was reinforced by three main factors (see Cohen, 1965; Matras, 1973). First, the potential marriage market was drastically reduced: 8 of the 22 villages in the Shefar-A'm region were destroyed as a result of the war, their inhabitants became either external or internal refugees. Second, the military government was established by the State of Israel in large areas of the Arab population, including Shefar-A'm, until 1966. This restricted the movement of the local population and further reinforced the localization process. Third, the economic and the administrative dependency between Shefar-A'm and the surrounding villages disappeared. This had significant social consequences in terms of decreasing the extra-local field of eligibles. In the pre-State period, economic relations provided wider opportunities for matchmaking by expanding the field of eligibles. We have identified 21 cases of extra-local marriages among Moslems during the period 1931-47 (25 percent of the total marriages). In 14 cases, the meeting between the families of the bride and the bridegroom was the result of economic relations which developed between families.

Several other sociodemographic factors contributed to the kinship structure concentration. Rapid natural increase contributed to hamula size as reflected in the number of its members within the same locality. Our data indicate that 82 percent of the Druze hamulas are considered relatively large in size (10000 persons and over), 68 percent of the Christians, 55 percent of local Moslems, and 25 percent of refugee Moslems.

A slight increase in the birth rate occurred in response to a decline in infant mortality after the establishment of the State. This increase affected the availability of mates among the hamulas by changing the balance in the sex ratio (Friedlander, Eisenbach and Goldscheider, 1979). (For more examples of the importance of the sex ratio on the marriage market see Dixon, 1971.) To illustrate this point, we compared the sex ratio among the Druze hamulas in the two main periods: before and after the establishment of the State of Israel. At the same time, we followed the cohorts in order to identify their type of marriage. During the five years selected in the course of the Mandatory Period (1930-35), the number of surviving children among all the Druze hamulas was 35 males and 42 females. The sex ratio was 83 males per 100 females (among small hamulas the sex ratio was 25:100). Among the females, one remained unmarried throughout, three were married outside the locality in the villages Daliet el-Carmel, Osofya and the Golan Heights, and thirty-five were married within the same locality. Among the males, one married a wife from Osofya and the rest were married within the locality. The total percentages of patrilineal marriage among the cohorts was 22 percent. During the five years examined after the establishment of the State (1960-65), the number of surviving children was 123 males and 126 females. The sex ratio increased to 95 males per 100 females. Among these cohorts, 46 females and 36 males had already married (the average age at marriage was 23 for grooms and 19 for brides). Of this number, 25 females compared to 18 males were married within the hamula, 20 females compared to 18 males were married outside the hamula within the same locality, and one female was married outside the locality. The total percentage of patrilineal endogamy was 52 percent. However, the percentages differ sharply when we take into account the hamula size--76 percent of the marriages among the two largest hamulas (500 persons and over) were patrilineal versus 25 percent among the small hamulas (less than 100 persons).

The hamula concentration was reinforced by the fact that little geographic movement took place and social areas were created within the locality based on hamula or kinship group affiliation. Usually in developing societies the surplus rural labor force migrates from traditional agricultural areas to urban areas seeking new job opportunities (see Goldscheider, 1983). The surplus labor force of the Arab minority in Israel generally, as well as in the local community resulted in a process of proletarianization in which most worked outside the original locality but continued to live there (see Rosenfeld, 1964). Thus, the Arab localities experienced latent urbanization. The process of migration to the nearby cities (Haifa, Acre, and Jaffa), which characterized Shefar-A'm during the late decades of the Mandatory Period, was restricted after the establishment of the State. In addition, movements within the locality created new neighborhoods based on hamula descent lines, as a result of the concentration of the hamula's lands in specific areas.

71

The various changes which occurred in the Arab minority in Israel, and in the local community specifically, created a new kinship structure among refugee Moslems unlike the classic definition of kinship structure based on biological relatedness (see Levy, 1965). Instead of biological relatedness to the great-grandfather, the new relatedness was linked to the name of the original village. Persons who came from Meār became Meāri (attached to Meār, rather than the hamula name), those from Damūn became Damūni, and those from Ruweis became Ruweisi. (All these villages were located in the western Galilee and were destroyed during the war of 1948.) The name of the original village replaced the name of the hamula, and the relationship among persons who belonged to the same original village became similar to the hamula solidarity. The hamula did not disappear or weaken, but some of its basic functions were transferred to the wider kinship structure based on locality. In this sense, the hamula was transformed and redefined. Similar evidence is derived from the case of the Vietnamese refugees in the United States. Their emphasis on kinship and the community is reflected in their redefinition of the community as one that refers "to a particular set of people bound together by actual, and possibly fictive, kinship ties" (see Hains, Rutherford, and Thomas, 1981).

As mentioned, the newly formed kinship group inside and outside the locality became the main unit in the marriage market. During the first decade, all the refugee marriages took place within the newly formed kinship group, 59 percent within the same group in the same locality, 25 percent within the same group outside the locality and only 16 percent within the same group and the same hamula. Furthermore, they tried to make marriage connections with local Moslems. During the 1980s, marriages between refugees and local Moslems constituted 30 percent of the total marriages of the refugees. Moreover, 70 percent of these marriages were in one direction: refugee male with local female. This pattern reflects the minority-majority relation which still exists between the locals and the refugees. Marriage connections with a local family mean greater social integration for the refugee. The asymmetric structural relation between groups is thereby related to an asymmetric marriage pattern.

The Political Role

Most studies agree that the political role of the hamula

became one of its major roles after the establishment of Israel (see Linenberg, 1971; Nakhleh, 1975; Habash, 1977; Abu-Gosh, 1972). The question remains whether this is a continuation of the hamula's status from the period preceding the establishment of Israel or has the political role of the hamula been reinforced. As noted earlier, studies have suggested no adequate answer for this question. Cohen (1965) distinguished three main periods in the hamula's political status. First was the musha period, in which the hamula played a crucial role in the communal land division and the protection of its members. In this period, the hamula emerged the central political group in the community life. The abolishment of the musha system as a result of land registration in the 1930s decreased drastically the hamula's economic role and increased the class differentiation within the hamula. This also resulted in the weakening of the hamula as a political group. The emergence of the Arab national organizations in that period reinforced this trend. After the establishment of Israel, there was a revival in the hamula's political role. The narrowing of the class differentiation as a result of the drastic economic change enabled many hamulas who were considered marginal to participate in the struggle over the local political system. In addition, the hamula emerged as a political unit because there was no alternative, since Arabs in Israel are not integrated in the Israeli national political system. This thesis has become controversial in later studies (see Al-Haj, 1979).

Shefar-A'm is an ideal place to trace the main trends in the hamula political role throughout the several periods, since it was among the first Arab localities in the northern part of Israel to be granted city rights and to be administered by an elected city council. In addition, as noted earlier, it includes all the representative groups among the Arabs in Israel. We examined the political role of the hamula by a longitudinal analysis of the municipal elections over a period of 70 years, beginning with the establishment of Shefar-A'm as a municipality in 1910. In addition, we analyzed the data obtained from the sample of detailed and in-depth interviews with some of the prominent leaders among the several groups in the community.

The appointment of the first city council in 1910 clearly reflected the gap in the economic position between Christians and Druze, on the one hand, and Moslems on the other. The regional governor (the Ottoman mudir) selected five Christians, one Druze, and no Moslems for the city council. The economic marginality of Moslems coincided with their political marginality, since membership in the city council was the exclusive right of large landowners and tax-payers (see Maoz, 1962). This appointed first council was only for a transitional period until the formation of an elected council.

Following a transitional period of four years, the first municipal elections were held in March 1915. Thirty-three citizens ran for the council: five Druze, eight Moslems, and twenty Christians. The elections were held over a period of three days in order to enable all franchized citizens who wished to cast their vote to reach the polls in time. The right to vote, however, was granted only to citizens 25 years of age and older who paid the minimum amount of municipal taxes. The latter condition deprived the low income classes - in this case the vast majority of the Moslem community - of the right to vote. In the course of these three days, 64 persons cast their ballot: 38 Christians, 14 Druze, and only 12 Moslems. Seven candidates were elected: one Druze, one Moslem, and five Christians. The district governor then appointed a Christian mayor from among the elected members.

The analysis of these elections revealed some interesting findings. The voting was personal, not based on lists. The candidates were representatives of extended families (dor), rather than hamulas (hamayil). Among the candidates, we identified several competitors who belonged to the same hamula: among the Moslems, Taha El-khatib, Abd-allah El-khatib, and El-sadiq Khatib belonged to the Khatib Hamula, while Ali Hamadi, Muhammad Hamadi, and Nemir Husein belonged to the El-Safafri hamula. Among the Christians, Tayeh Abu-Rahmeh, and Mansur Abu-Rahmeh belonged to the hamula of Abu-Rahmeh, while Dawud Talhami and Najeeb Talhami belonged to the Talhami hamula. Among the Druze, Saleh Layyan and Salim Layyan belonged to the Layyan hamula. Three out of the seven elected candidates belonged to small hamulas. Karam El-Jubran, who received the majority of votes (46 votes), belonged to a very small hamula composed of only one extended family.

These facts indicate that the extended family, rather than the hamula, was the main political unit. Unlike Cohen's conclusion, we found that class differentiation divided the hamula even before the abolition of the musha system. The allocation of the musha lands was made according to extended family, not hamula, affiliation. The political system in the community was based on a religious balance dominated by Christians. Among each religious group, the community leaders came from the wealthy extended households.

This situation continued during the Mandatory Period,

although the end of the first mayor's term of office in 1933 revealed that there were conflicts even within the Christian community. Two Christian candidates ran for the office of mayor: one of them the son of the mukhtar of the Catholic community, the other a well-known Maronite who had been a member of the council since the first elections. The Catholic candidate won the election. It should be noted that these were the only elections held in Shefar-A'm during the entire pre-Israel period. After the first elections, the members of the council, including the chairman, were re-appointed by general agreement of the communities (tazkiyeh).

The traditional status quo in the council was preserved until the end of the first decade of Statehood, with communal affiliation and landed property as the principal keys to the town's administration. This was reflected in the appointment of the city council in 1951, which was composed of three Christians, three Druze, and two Moslems, in addition to the Christian mayor.

The sociodemographic and economic changes noted earlier have changed the status system in the community from a status structure determined by landownership and other economic resources to a status structure determined by group size and the ability to form tight networks. The hamula has become a strong social and political unit because of the increase in size and, most importantly because of the narrowing--or the disappearance--of class differentiation among the hamula members. In addition, the overall proletarianization process has narrowed the class differentiation among the several groups in the community (see Cohen, 1965). As in other places (see Tamari, 1981) this has resulted in the emergence of new hamulas, composed of numbers who had hitherto been placed on the lowest stratum of the social ladder, as competitors for the local political system.

In the 1969 elections, Moslems supported their own list of candidates, which was composed of local and in-migrant Moslems. The Druze supported two hamula-based lists and the Christians supported three hamula-based lists. The communist's list was the only one which received the support of different hamulas and religious groups. Out of the nine elected council members, three were affiliated with the list of the Moslems, two with the Druze, three with the lists of the Christians and one with the list of the communists. For the first time, Moslems won the post of Mayor by their coalition with the Druze representatives.

The cohesion of the Moslem community prompted a similar move among the Christians and Druze, each of whom presented communal lists in the elections of 1973. But this communal unity did not last. It disintegrated before the next elections, four years later, because of fierce internal conflicts between the hamulas of the Christian and Druze communities. Paradoxically, the Moslem communal list succeeded in maintaining its solidarity because of the breakdown in its hamulas. The weakening of the Moslem hamulas and the considerable strengthening of the Druze and Christian hamulas were due to the same sociodemographic factors which were discussed earlier. First, the central position of the Moslem hamulas was weakened because of the departure of large numbers of Moslems families who settled in the Arab countries. Second, the influx of internal refugees (almost all of them Moslems), coming as single families or as sections of hamulas, did much to strengthen the collective character of the Moslem community at the expense of its hamula character. These refugees pressed for communal unity because such unity increased their chances to influence, as a group, the general social structure of the settlement, while a division into hamulas would likely diminish their power to advance their own interests. In effect, the priorities within the other religious groups were reversed. Whereas the Christians and the Druze moved from loyalty to the community to loyalty to the neighborhood and the hamulas, the Moslems moved from loyalty to the hamulas, extended families, and neighborhood to loyalty to the community.

The inter-religious political agreements and covenants also assumed a different character. From the establishment of the first city council until the end of the first decade after the rise of Israel, the Druze kept their agreement with the Christians and thus helped to preserve the balance in the settlement in which the Christians had both political hegemony and economic power. The mid-1960s saw the first signs of a change and a reapproachment between the Druze and the Moslems. This process reached its climax in the late 1960s with the political upheaval brought about by the unity of the Moslem community and its coalition with the Druze, a coalition which has persisted till the present day. In the recent 1983 municipal elections, a Christian list, representing virtually the entire local Christian community, joined the Moslem-Druze coalition. The new coalition thus comprises all the religious groups; it is headed by a Moslem mayor who has two Druze deputies and a Christian acting mayor. This coalition was formed on the basis of the "communal balance" and is acceptable to the overwhelming majority of the local population, as it consists of eight of the council's eleven members.

The recent elections confirmed an interesting development. The focus of inter-communal strife has shifted from between the religious groups to the hamulas and to sectors within each of the religious groups. During the recent elections, the principal contests were between lists of candidates within each of these sectors. Among the Moslems, for example, the competition was between two lists of candidates: a major list representing the community at large and a new list made up of hamulas and neighborhoods. The Christians also had two lists: the traditional one claiming to represent the community and a new list which defeated the former and subsequently joined the existing coalition. The Druze, too, campaigned with two lists: the traditional one representing the entire community and a new list of young people from all the hamulas. The latter, however, did not obtain the required quota. These contests within the communities will undoubtedly have far-reaching repercussions in the future for the division of power in the town.

Throughout all the municipal election campaigns after the establishment of Israel, the political activity was centered around local lists based on religious hamula affiliation. Excluding the communist list, the local elections lacked any ideological meaning. In Shefar-A'm as well as the other Arab localities in Israel, there is no direct participation of the national parties in the local elections. The national political parties, all of them Zionist, support indirectly the local lists in order to gain their mutual aid in the parliamentary elections (see Landau, 1972; Abu-Gosh, 1972; Linenberg, 1971).

The Economic Role

The economic role is less prominent than the other hamula roles. Unlike Cohen's conclusion (1965), we found that the hamula has never been an economic unit even under the musha system (the communal land). As noted earlier, the musha lands in Shefar-A'm were divided between the three religious groups every five years. Analysis of the division in a typical year (1914) revealed that the internal division among each religious group was made according to the key extended families rather than the hamulas. For example, the lands of the Christian community were divided into 64 unequal plots, one plot for each certain extended household (dar). Further examination of the names of the extended households revealed that they did not encompass the entire household among the hamulas. Within the same hamula there were some households who received large plots, some received modest or small plots, and some did not receive any plots.

77

It appears that the criteria for land allocation was the period of settlement in the locality and the possession of other kinds of property (mulk). It may be assumed that personal effects were also involved. This resulted in class differentiation among the hamula members. The abolishment of the musha system may have increased, rather than created, the class differentiation among the hamula.

The major economic role of the hamula was reflected in the mutual aid system which developed among the hamula members. This system sometimes remained only a potential source which was not exploited, but yet it did not lose its value. The mutual aid among the hamula members was periodic, not a day-to-day occurrence. It was observed mainly during the harvest season and during the most expensive events in the life cycle, e.g., marriage and building a new house. Events such as blood feuds also necessitated hamula cooperation. If one of the hamula members was found guilty of murder or of violating the family honor of another hamula, all the members of the first hamula claimed responsibility. Every household affiliated with the hamula contributed his portion to the payment of the ransom. The available documents covering the period 1920-82 indicated ten cases (one murder and 9 connected with family honor) in which the hamula members were required to pay a ransom. One of the informants indicated that in the case of the murder, the hamula was not able to pay the blood money. Eventually, the amount was collected by the people of the neighborhood.

The mutual aid was much more prominent during the harvest season than at other times. Evidence of this was found in several personal documents and diaries. Some hamulas even formed a fixed schedule for the mutual aid. In one of the diaries (1935) a farmer reported:

> In the early May we met in our Uncle's house in order to coordinate the hamula work in the harvesting. We decided to begin with the fields of Abu-Saleh; they were ripe and most urgent. After the completion of this work we will move to the fields of Abu-Ali, finally we will work together in my fields.

We traced the available reports in these diaries for four years (until 1938). A similar arrangement among the hamula members was found throughout the entire period. The mutual aid during the harvest seasons was observed in particular among the modest and the small farmers. No evidence was found to indicate this

78

phenomenon among the large landowners. Maybe this is because large landowners were able to hire wage laborers if needed.

The hamula's role as a potential source for aid in the case of troubles or distress was also of major importance. Under the agrarian system, the small landowners or the landless suffered the most from lack of social security. There were no formal institutions to provide security to them under conditions of drought or other unexpected troubles. The hamula members were the only source at hand. This was demonstrated in a hamula proverb "in māl fik el-dahir aleik bil-ahil" (if you are in calamity, turn to your relatives).

Currently the economic role of the hamula is negligible. This fact was reflected in the answers of the respondents to the question about the resources for their loans or any other financial support. Only nine percent indicated that they received financial support from their kinship group, while another five percent indicated they received support from their neighbors and friends. The overwhelming majority (86 percent) noted that they received support from their employer, the government or other formal institutions (Housing Ministry, bank, etc.).

Our findings do not support the conclusion of Ben-Shahar and Marx (1972) that the hamula still functions as a framework for cooperation and therefore has impeded the development of a formal cooperative system in the Arab localities in Israel. At present, the economic role of the hamula is mainly potential rather than actual. Several respondents noted that it was important to retain the mutual aid among the hamula members during crisis or unexpected troubles. However, the importance of such aid has decreased because of the availability of a formal social security system.

Modernization Factors versus Sociodemographic Factors

How did modernization factors affect the structure of the hamula? Was their effect greater than that of sociodemographic factors?

Sociodemographic factors were juxtaposed with modernization factors in order to determine both of their effects on hamula orientation at the normative and behavioral levels. Sociodemographic factors include age, sex, hamula size, the existence of hamula leadership, neighborhood group composition, and period of settlement for refugees. Modernization factors include formal education, place of employment, type of employment (domestic, non-domestic), mass media exposure, contact with the Jewish population, formal organizational affiliation, psychological modernity, preferred family planning, and attitudes towards women's status. Correlations among the sociodemographic variables indicate that hamula size was the most effective variable. Among modernization factors there was no one main variable. Three of the variables were equally important: formal education, mass media exposure, and preferred family planning. Since no considerable differences were identified among the several religious groups, our analysis will relate to the groups as a whole.

The findings in Table 3.2 point to several major conclusions. hamula continues to be a major influence on the social and the political behavioral level, while its influence at the normative level has drastically decreased. The findings suggest a glaring gap between norms and actual behavior. While 38 percent were married within the hamula, only 7.6 percent still approve the traditional, conventional norms underlying the patrilineal system. Moreover, 34.6 percent supported hamula -based lists in the local elections, while only 15 percent approved hamula loyalty as an ideal. However, this gap does not emerge in the economic role of the hamula, which diminished at the normative as well as the behavioral level. Only six percent of the respondents considered their hamula affiliation an important component of their socioeconomic status, and only nine percent received economic aid from their hamula. Sociodemographic factors accounted for a significant part of the explanation of the behavioral patterns. While sociodemographic factors are associated with the behavioral level, modernization and sociodemographic factors combine to affect norms. There appears to be a monotonic relationship among the several categories of attitudes according to hamula size. However, this pattern does not appear as clearly at the behavioral level.

Kinship group concentration, accompanied by a lack of geographic movement inside and outside the locality, creates a dynamic relationship between the kinship group and its members. On the one hand, it supports the control of the lineage group over its members. The relationship between the individual and his kinship group is perceived as stable, continuous, and permanent. Therefore, individuals have to take the hamula expectations into account, to some extent. On the other hand, kinship group members seek to take advantage of their kinship group size in their adjustment to social and the political possibilities. This occurs both, in terms of the internal relationship within the

TABLE 6.1

FAMILY SIZE AND FAMILY PLANNING AMONG RELIGIOUS, LOCAL,
AND MIGRATORY GROUPS, SHEFAR-A'M,
1981*

	Local Groups			In-migrant Group		
	Christians	Moslems	Inmigrant Druze	Druze Moslems	Druze Moslems	El-Jabal
Family Size Actual						
Small family (0-2 children)	29.0	23.0	21.0	16.0	17.0	22.0
Moderate family (3-4 children)	47.0	39.0	36.0	36.0	39.0	38.0
Large family (5 children and over)	24.0	38.0	43.0	48.0	44.0	40.0
Total	100.0	100.0	100.0	100.0	100.0	100.0
Ideal						
Small family	17.9	17.0	16.1	11.8	16.0	16.5
Moderate family	68.6	67.5	67.2	67.2	69.8	68.5
Large family	13.5	15.5	16.7	21.0	14.2	15.0
Total	100.0	100.0	100.0	100.0	100.0	100.0
N	434	256	248	229	18	1085
Family Planning Actual						
None	5.5	7.0	10.0	14.0	9.8	11.0
Partial	55.0	64.0	69.0	72.0	71.0	61.0
Full	39.5	29.0	21.0	14.0	19.2	28.0
Total	100.0	100.0	100.0	100.0	100.0	100.0
N = 120						
Preferred						
None	4.0	13.0	11.0	16.0	5.0	12.0
Partial	25.9	19.0	21.0	42.0	24.0	34.0
Full	70.1	68.0	68.5	42.0	71.0	64.0
Total	100.0	100.0	100.0	100.0	100.0	100.0
N = 120						

*Family size refers to the spouses after 10 years of marriage. The data are de-
rived from the comprehensive survey. Family planning refers to all the spouses.
The data is derived from the detailed interviews.

kinship group itself, and in terms of interaction between the kinship group and its milieu on the communal level.

Neither structural nor psychological modernity led to modernizing changes in actual behavior. Modernization variables suggested no significant distinction between hamula oriented and non-hamula oriented types of behavior. Nevertheless, as reflected by the relationship between modernization variables and normative level, modernization processes contributed to profound normative change and drastically minimized the traditional ideological base of the kinship structure. The modernization changes noted earlier have resulted in the conception that an individual's attainments and social status are not the by-product of his hamula affiliation but are the results of his personal efforts. Therefore loyalty and other ideological commitments to the hamula per se have become less important. This trend is reinforced by increased exposure to modern forces such as mass media, contact with Jews, etc. which assign prestige and social mobility to education and technical skills rather than to affiliation to descent groups (see Avitsour, 1978).

Currently, hamula functions are based on pragmatic requirements rather than on cultural or ideological commitments. Lack of alternative patterns of actual behavior provides the basis for the conservation and reinforcement of the kinship structure. The macro sociodemographic and the economic processes created a pragmatic base for patrilineal endogamy since the extra-lineal marriage market decreased while the field of eligibles within the hamula increased. Analysis of the political and the economic hamula roles supports our conclusion.

Contrary to the Jewish majority, most of the lists in the local elections are based on hamulas or other descent groups, rather than on national parties (see Nakhleh, 1975; Abu-Gosh, 1972). The Arab minority in Israel is considered a cultural-religious minority and not a national minority. Therefore, the formation of Arab national parties is prohibited (see Sabri, 1973). Under the available political possibilities, the kinship group functions as a political unit not because it is well organized politically, but because of the lack of political alternatives (see Habash, 1977; Cohen, 1965).

The economic role of the hamula (unlike the political and social roles) is negligible. Changes in socioeconomic processes have provided alternative resources for the support of the hamula. The economic transformation which led to economic dependency on the Jewish sector eliminated the collective base of domestic or other kinship group economic activity. Individual economic activity became dominant and individual achievement was emphasized. Moreover, the availability of alternative formal economic sources decreased the need for kinship group support.

In sum, our analysis has demonstrated the importance of examining the kinship structure within a broader framework which takes into consideration biological relatedness as well as social interaction. Our analysis has shown that the hamula status is determined both by the relationships within the community and between the community and external forces. The roles of the hamula are based on pragmatic requirements and constraints, rather than on ideological and cultural commitments. We suggest that the effect of modernization on the kinship structure is diverse, rather than uniform.

Generally speaking, our findings support the argument that the Arab kinship structure has been reinforced since the establishment of Israel (see Cohen, 1965; Rosenfeld, 1972; Nakhleh, 1975). However, some modifications to this conclusion need to be made. The status of the kinship structure consists of diverse phases and is not uniform. While the social and political roles of the hamula have been reinforced, the economic role has decreased drastically. In addition, a conspicuous change has occurred in the ideological-normative basis of the hamula. Unlike Cohen's conclusion (1965), we suggest that throughout the periods preceding the establishment of Israel, the most dominant family structure was the extended family, rather than the hamula. The extended family emerged as the main familial unit, not only economically, but socially and politically as well. We may conclude that the hamula dominance is, to a large extent, an outcome of the conditions of Statehood and the position of the Arab community within Israel.

What are the implications of these conclusions for the other familial units--the extended family and the nuclear family? Does the diversification found in the kinship structure indicate a similar direction in the extended family? These questions will be examined in the next chapter.

4

The Extended Family

Several studies have emphasized the importance of the extended family in agrarian and nonindustrial economies. The extended family has served as an economic unit as well as a social and political framework for its members. Under these circumstances, the nuclear family was submerged within the extended unit, where the control over the family property and resources was concentrated in the hands of the patriarch father (see Rosenfeld, 1980; Kanaana, 1975; Lutfiyya, 1970). The extended family structure affected the decision making of all the family members, even those decisions concerning married sons and their own families. Therefore, changes in fertility, women's status, modes of consumption and other aspects of family life have been linked to changes in the extended family and in the nature of the relationships among its members (see Caldwell, 1977, 1982; Freedman, Chang, and Sun, 1982). We found it of major importance to analyze the extended family, its changing characteristics and roles, as one base for our understanding of the family life styles in Shefar-A'm and the dynamics of the interaction among the several familial units.

The formal definition of the extended, or the joint, family is: a familial unit composed of three generations, the father, the mother, the unmarried children, one or more of the married sons and their wives and children. Sometimes the extended family includes as well a single uncle or aunt (see Granquist, 1935; Rosenfeld, 1964; Berger, 1962). Several elements have been identified as the main characteristics of the extended family: common residence, property, common workshop or other economic base, kitchen, patriarchal authority, and mutual commitments among the family members (see Gore, 1965; Antoun, 1968; Rosenfeld, 1968; Lutfiyya, 1970). These elements can be classified into two main interrelated groups: structural and associative elements. Structural elements include coresidence and functioning of the extended family as a unit of production and consumption. The associative elements are defined in terms of "identification with and responsibility for the well being of all the members of that unit" (Kanaana, 1975:17). This definition implies that the associative elements are not conditioned by the existence of the structural elements. We may hypothesize that the family members may continue to identify with the original extended family, to keep close relations and contact and mutual aid, even without the common residence, consumption, and joint economic base.

It has generally been argued that the extended family is a traditional structure typical of agrarian society. In the wake of the modernization process, this extended unit is expected to disappear and to be replaced by the nuclear family based on interests of the couple and their children (see Gulick, 1968; Caldwell, 1977). One assumption often associated with the modernization approach is that the process of family nucleation experienced by developed societies is inevitable and therefore developing societies will sooner or later experience the same process. As Kanaana (1975:5) noted, "the belief that the extended family is incompatible with modernity is so widely accepted that many studies do not even question the effect of modernity on the extended family but take for granted that the extended family as an institution will disappear from the Middle East in the face of advancing modernity." However, research conducted in several developing societies has shown the coexistence of the extended family with conspicuous modernization changes (see Gore, 1965; Freedman, Chang and Sun, 1982; Kanaana, 1975).

What elements in the extended family are first to change in the process of modernization? How are class factors related to modernization? The answers to these questions have not been clear. Some have argued that the nature of the relationships among the extended family members have changed more rapidly than the structural elements, reflected mainly in coresidence within the extended household. Research conducted in Taiwan has noted that there was conspicuous modernization in most of the elements were in the extended family; the coresidence pattern was merely lagging behind so that more complete modernization was only a matter of time (Freedman, Chang, and Sun, 1982:410). Others have argued that the fragmentation of the extended family in terms of coresidence was the primary result of economic changes and the modernization process. Paradoxically, these processes have retained and even reinforced the associative elements in the extended family as reflected in the social interaction and mutual commitments among the family members. Perhaps the associative elements have been reinforced because modernization processes have not been strong enough to provide alternative patterns for the extended relations (see Gore, 1965; Rosenfeld, 1968; Kanaana, 1975).

Another controversial point relates to the linkage between class and family structures. Some have argued that the upper class was the first to adjust to the modernization process and thus to undergo family nucleation (see Aries, 1971; Goode, 1963). Others have indicated an opposite pattern with the continuation of the extended family structure among the upper and the middle classes. The poor, landless, or tenant-farmer father could not maintain an extended family for long, "since he had neither the material means of supporting married sons and their families, nor those that could provide him with the sole authority to dictate their future" (Rosenfeld, 1968:734).

In this chapter, these controversial points will be addressed systematically. The several elements of the extended family will be examined, currently and over time. Family structure will be analyzed along with changes in modes of production and with modernization factors. Through longitudinal analysis we shall be able to trace the changes in the several elements of the extended family and the dynamics of the interaction among them. Moreover, the analysis will furnish the basis for examining the starting point of the transition from an extended to a nuclear family unit. Our major questions are: Is there a typical extended family structure or a diversity of types? What are the main changes in the extended family over time and which elements are first to undergo change? What specific aspects of modernization relate to changes in the extended family? What is the effect of the community religious structure on the status of the extended family?

In the community under research, the extended household was the main familial unit until the late years of the Mandatory Period, and, to some extent, until the last years of the first decade after the establishment of Israel. Examination of the several elements of the extended family revealed that they were diverse and generally associated with the modes of production and the class structure. There was no single typical extended family, either under the agrarian economy or after the proletarianization process was underway.

As anticipated, until the last years of the Mandatory Period, there were four main socioeconomic strata in Shefar-A'm: the merchants and the business owners, the large landowners, the modest farmers, and the small farmers and the landless. Each is linked with a unique type of family structure, although the several types also had common characteristics. The merchants and some of the Christian large landowners maintained an extended family in terms of residence, consumption, and other associative elements. Nevertheless, the family was not a production unit. Almost all the business shops were handled by one family member, the father or the eldest son. The other male members in the family developed different skills, in particular white collar job skills. Most of the teachers, clerks, and other governmental officers came from this stratum. In most cases, the sons lived with their parents until marriage when they moved to an independent household. The authority was concentrated in the father's hands, because he had control over most of the family property. After the marriage, the son became independent economically and in terms of residence. He received his share of the inheritance only after the father's death.

A similar situation was found among some of the Christian landowners. The analysis of the diaries of some landowners revealed that the father, sometimes with the help of the elder son, usually supervised the work on the family lands. Most of the work was carried out by hired laborers or by sharecroppers, where the landowner provided the land, the seeds, and the work animals and the sharecropper provided the labor and received one-fifth to one-fourth of the production (see Rosenfeld, 1964). The available documents do not reveal the involvement of family members in the field work. The family property was usually maintained intact until the father's death. Only in two cases, out of several hundreds, were the lands divided among the sons during the father's lifetime. The informants indicated, however, that the land division was only formal, in order to ease the taxes on the lands. In reality they remained integrated.

Some of the large landowners among the Christians, and all of the large landowners among the Druze and the Moslems maintained an extended family, similar to the modest farmers. This comprised all the elements of the extended family noted earlier. However, the large landowners differed from the modest farmers in that the family members of the modest landowners were much more active economically than those of the large landowners. Modest farmers had enough lands for their own livelihood but not enough to allow them to hire extra labor, except during the harvest season.

A typical example of the extended family among the modest farmers was described in one of the farmer's diaries. He reported daily the main work conducted on his land and the people involved. It should be noted that the farmer did not mention the work done by the small children. This may be because the children's work was perceived only as supplementary and not as a main contribution. In what follows we will summarize the main work conducted throughout the year of 1935. All the references to sons are to adult children.

January: The father and his two sons ploughed the fields and planted wheat and barley.

February: They continued at the same work of January.

March: The father, the son, and the mother prepared the field and planted chickpeas. The father and the two sons ploughed around the olive trees.

April: At the beginning of the month, the father and his two sons started to prepare the land for summer crops. Some plots were planted with watermelon and marrow (the mother also shared in this work). April 28 - May 5 so the weather was very hot, no one worked the land.

May: April 6 - May 14, the father and one of his sons planted sesame, tomato and marrow. May 15 - May 31, the harvest season started--the father, the sons, and the mother took part. In addition, they hired two workers.

June: They started hauling grain from the fields to the threshing floor, where the economic activity was concentrated during the month.

July: The threshing lasted until mid July. July 15 - July 30, the farmer had a time to rest and to make his calculation as to how to divide the crops--some for the payment of debts, some for his own consumption, and some for the market.

August: The work was concentrated in the watermelon fields. At the end of August, they began marketing watermelon to Haifa and Acre (the father and his sons).

September: Olive harvest--all the family members took part in addition to one hired worker.

October: The end of the olive harvest.

November: A break between seasons. A lot of social activities were reported (participating in wedding ceremonies, mutual visits, etc.).

December: The seasonal agricultural activity started again. The father and the two sons ploughed and prepared the lands for winter crops.

A calculation of the work days revealed that the father and his two sons worked intensively, and sometimes extensively, for 298 days throughout the year. The mother contributed 121 work days, most of them during the harvest seasons. In addition, she handled the housework and took care of the children.[1]

The extended household maintained by the modest farmers was the most dominant form of family structure. Its main components were: coresidence and functioning as a production as well as a consumption unit. The associative elements among the family members were assured by the father's control of the family property. All the family members were dependent economically, and to a great extent socially, on the patriarch father. The father financed the bride price and the other marriage costs for the sons. Family fragmentation usually occurred after the father's death. In some cases, even then, the sons continued to maintain the extended household and to retain the land integrity in order to keep the convenience of agricultural work (see Rosenfeld, 1968).

The lowest stratum (small farmers and landless) apparently maintained the same extended family as the other strata although an in-depth examination showed large differences among them, mainly in the nature of and the basis for the extended family. It should be noted that it was most difficult to obtain data about family life styles among the lowest stratum, since they did not

----

[1] The women's role in the extended family will be discussed in detail in the next chapter.

write diaries or kept any written reports. The vast majority of the farmers who belonged to this stratum were illiterate. Therefore, we relied heavily on interviews with the key informants along with some available documents obtained from the municipality. One of the informants, who belonged to this strata noted:

> Our life was a mixture of hard work and poverty. The small plot of land I inherited from my father was not sufficient to sustain my family which was composed of ten persons. I had to work as a laborer on the Christian's and the Druze's farms. The large landowners could support work for the whole year. At the harvest season, my wife and the three children worked with me for the same employer, every one had his work. We used to start working before the sunshine and to return home after the sunset... We received our payment in money, and sometimes by crop. I had the responsibility for the income and the livelihood of the family. I had also the responsibility for supporting the marriage of my sons. When the first son was maried he continued to live with us at the same house. We divided one of the two rooms we possessed. This was used as a bedroom for the new couple. The other facilities continued to be common. When the second son was married we had no room for him. We added a room in our backyard. The third son was married one year before the war (the Israel-Arab War in 1948). He lived apart in a house which was given by his employer. Later, he left the work in agriculture and began to work as a wage laborer in Kfar-Ata (a nearby Jewish town). Although he had commitment towards us, he rarely gave a part of his wage for the family income. He took care only of his family livelihood, almost with no assistance from us.

The household among the lowest stratum had all the elements of an extended family. Nevertheless, the nature of the relationship among its members was completely different than the other types noted before. Among the lowest stratum the extended family served as a labor unit not a production unit. The family owned almost no property and nothing was expected to be inherited. The sons continued to live with the extended household, mainly because of the lack of alternatives. Few could live apart after their marriage and maintain independent households. This structure was maintained out of family necessity not because of family interest (economic interest). Therefore, the extended structure continued as long as necessary. When one of the sons found an alternative of establishing an independent household, he generally left the extended household with the approval of the other members, since this reduced the burden of the extended household.

Continuity and Change after the Establishment of Israel

Several changes occurred after the establishment of Israel which brought about drastic changes in the structural elements of the extended family. Fewer changes were observed in the associative elements. Changes in the family structure were to a large extent the outcome of changes in occupation and modes of production. Therefore, the continuity of the previous economic structure until the last years of the first decade after the establishment of Israel retained the extended family structure as well. The first decade may be defined as a period of transition. During this period, economic changes and alterations in family structure developed. These emerged clearly in the second decade. Familial changes, however, lagged behind the rapid economic changes.

The economic transformation resulted in conspicuous changes in the modes of dependency: from intercommunal to external dependency (see Chapter 2). This affected several elements of the extended family. Sons became less dependent on their fathers. Fewer workers were needed for the residual agriculture because of the reduction in the size of lands and the mechanization of agriculture. Unlike the agrarian period, the fragmentation of the family was not conditioned by the division of the property after the father's death. In many cases the inheritance was divided in the father's lifetime. The marginality of land as a base of economic existence decreased its value as a means by which the patriarch father could control the family members. Moreover, the father did not need to keep control of the property in order to secure his future in time of old age. This was secured through the social security system supported by the state (e.g., social insurance, income insurance). In addition, the households in which the father had some property to divide declined drastically. Over half of the respondents reported that their fathers had nothing to divide. This is true in particular among the Moslems, in-migrant groups (refugees, Bedouins, and Druze El-Jabal), and the households among all the religious groups who were small farmers or landless during the pre-1948 period.

The data obtained from the comprehensive survey show that in the 1980s about 85 percent of the households are nuclear in terms of residence and economic activities. Only 15 percent can be defined as extended according to two or more elements, out of the five elements of the extended family noted earlier. Among the extended households, nine percent are composed of married couples (without children or with one or two children) living with parents for less than five years after their marriage and six percent include married couples (with children) living with parents for more than five years after their marriage.

Similar findings emerge from several studies conducted in Arab communities in Israel as well as in Arab countries. Baruch (1966) noted that in the 1960s, only 20 percent of the households in Nazareth were extended. A continuous trend of separated residence of married couples was clearly observed. We may assume a further decline in the extended household since that period. A study conducted on the changes in agriculture in the Arab villages in Israel and the West Bank noted that only ten percent of the households could be defined as extended (Arnon and Raviv, 1980). This pattern was documented also by a representative survey conducted on the Arab population in Israel. It was noted that in the 1980s, only 12.8 percent of the couples lived in an extended household (Smooha, 1984). A similar picture emerges in Jordan. Antoun (1972) noted that only 19 percent of the households in Kafr-Alma could be considered extended. Most of the households in this study were defined in terms of their common residence, not their function as production unit. Only one-third of them had a common economic basis.

In Shefar-A'm, a rapid trend of structural fragmentation of the extended family was observed. This was reflected in the answers of the couples who still resided with the extended household. In response to the question "why did you not move to a separate residence?" 45 percent reported that they were in the process of building their own house and would move after its completion. In most cases, residence with the extended household was the outcome of economic constraints and was not a voluntary pattern reflecting values. Among the couples living currently with extended households, 75 percent completely disapprove extended residence, 15 percent prefer independent residence but to some extent approve extended residence, and only 10 percent approve such residence.

It is remarkable that the change in the extended family structure is ubiquitous and not restricted to certain groups or to those who can be defined as modern. Overall, there are no considerable differences among the several groups in the community in terms of the existence of extended households. The percentage of the extended households is: 17 percent among the Druze, 13 percent among local Christians and local Moslems, 11 percent among in-migrant Moslems and 7 percent among Druze El-Jabal.

No relationship was found between residence in an extended household and the several factors of individual modernity. Table 4.1 shows clearly that the main components of westernization, mass media, education, and contact with an agent of westernization (i.e., the Jewish population), do not distinguish between those who live in nuclear households and those who still reside in extended households.

Despite the conspicuous rapid change in the structural elements of the extended family, the associative elements are still strong. Our findings support the argument that the structural elements of the extended family are the first to change in the modernization process. The associative elements and the extended relationships among family members are preserved even after the family nucleation occurs in terms of residence, economic function, and consumption (see Rosenfeld, 1968; Kanaana, 1975). As Gore noted, "the existence of nuclear household is, in itself, not a sufficient indication of change in family living. It is possible that individuals who live in nuclear households have attitudes and characteristics of the joint family" (Gore, 1965:212). In Shefar-A'm, the advanced modernization process has not resulted in the weakening of the extended relationships among family members. They are strongly observed on several occasions, as reflected in the identification of individuals with the extended family as well as in practical commitments and aid. The practical relationships are most clearly expressed during the most expensive events of the life cycle: marriage and building a new house.

The psychological continuity of the extended family is reflected in the perpetuation of the father's name by his sons. Usually one of the married sons (often the eldest) calls his elder child after his father. Examination of the names in the community reveals that in many cases a name is repeated twice throughout three generations, such as: Ahmad Ali Ahmad, Salim Karim Salim, Ábed Saleh Ábed, etc. In addition, some of the extended family names have replaced the names of the hamulas to reflect more commitment and identification with the extended family. A person from outside the community who is not aware of the hamula names in the community may be misled. He may

TABLE 4.1

RESIDENCE WITH EXTENDED HOUSEHOLD BY INDIVIDUAL
MODERNITY FACTORS, SHEFAR-A'M, 1982

| | Type of Residence | | |
Modernization Factors	Extended Household	Nuclear Household	Total
Education			
No education-primary	16.1	83.9	100.0
High school-higher education	14.6	85.4	100.0
Degree of contact with Jews			
Extensive or none	16.1	83.9	100.0
Intensive	13.0	87.0	100.0
Mass media exposure			
Low	13.5	86.5	100.0
Moderate	17.0	83.0	100.0
High	15.0	85.0	100.0

mistakenly think that two people come from different hamulas when in fact they belong to the same hamula. One of them may have used the extended family name instead of the hamula name. This phenomenon is observed among the three religious groups. Among Moslems we can find the names Nemir instead of Husein, Sadiq (Khatib); among Christians, Bŭlus (Abu-Rās), Muneeb (Ilias); among Druze, El-Hasan (Khneifis), El-Salim (Hassūn).

Several factors combine to induce the continuity of the relationships and the mutual commitments among family members. Parents, who have lost a great amount of their economic authority as a result of structural changes, have a special interest in the continuity of the sons' commitment to the household. This is the only way to have some affect on them and to compensate for their lost authority. The sons also have a major interest in the continuity of these relationships as a means of providing for their social security. This is especially important where there is a lack of social security outside the community due to the rapid economic and political changes which occurred after the establishment of Israel resulting in the total dependency on the Jewish dominant sector. In this sense, close relationships with family members and with their potential and actual aid constitute a major source of the individual's social security (see Rosenfeld, 1972; Kanaana, 1975).

Types of Contemporary Extended Families

By analyzing the main types of extended families currently in Shefar-A'm, we can delineate their main characteristics and compare them with those of the agrarian period. For this purpose, the extended family structure was examined in two stages. First, the main types of the extended family were identified by in-depth interviews and conversations with key informants along with participant observation. This revealed three main types: the business extended family, the agricultural extended family, and the extended family of residence. Second, three typical households (cases) were selected to exemplify the different types. In depth interviews were conducted with the main persons in each household: the father, the mother, and the elder son along with his wife. Informal conversations were conducted as well with other family members.

The Business Extended Family. The business extended family is based on domestic business managed by the father or the elder brother with the help of the other brothers. The duration of common residence with the extended family among sons differs: It is usually longest for the elder son, while the younger sons leave the household immediately after their marriage. The business continues to be common even after the father's death and despite the separated residence.

Case 1. The father originally worked in agriculture on his own lands during the Mandatory Period and the first years after the establishment of Israel. Later, he sold part of his lands but continued to work in agriculture. The elder son finished elementary school and began to work as a mechanic in the industrial area near Haifa (Mephratz). He worked several years as a wage laborer until he became a skilled worker. He decided to run his own garage, and his father supported him and funded the purchase of an appropriate workshop and equipment. This became the family business. The income from the business was deposited in the bank under the father's name. After the father's death, the responsibility for the family business was transferred to the elder brother, who had already married. He continued to live with the family and retained the common coresidence and consumption patterns. However, the wife of the elder brother only served her husband. She refused to work for the other family members. Even some of the household tasks assigned together were left to the mother-in-law and her unmarried daughter.

After the daughter's marriage, great pressure was put on the wife of the elder brother to handle the household needs and to take care of not only her husband but also the other family members. This was the onset of extensive conflict between the wife and the mother-in-law. It accelerated after the birth of the first grandson. The mother-in-law began to intervene in everything concerning the nursing of the child. The wife spared no effort to convince her husband to build a separate house, far from the extended family residence. "I strongly wanted to be independent," said the wife. But the husband refused because such a step would divide the family and the business. Moreover, the social pressure in the community played an important role. The husband said, "I did not want the people in my town to say that we could not maintain the integrity of our family, even for a few years after the death of our father." This situation lasted until the birth of the second grandson. "I was exhausted," said the wife, "to take care of two children, the husband, and the other family members is not a simple task." The husband also wanted "some privacy and independence." He started to build his house in the new neighborhood on family lands. One year later they moved to the new house. The older three brothers built separate houses near their elder brother before their marriages. The costs of the houses, the marriages, and other expenses were covered from the common account of the family. After the marriage, each received a monthly payment to cover his own economic needs. The residence and the consumption separated, but the business continued to be common.

The business extended family is a new familial type which includes traditional as well as new elements. Like the traditional extended family, the business family function as a production unit based mainly on a domestic labor force. It is extended in term of residence and consumption for a certain period. The father or the elder brother is the central source of authority. But unlike the traditional extended family, this type involves a new sort of authority division among the family members. It is based mainly on economic considerations, rather than traditional patriarchy. Unlike the traditional extended family, in this type the separation in residence and consumption does not imply a parallel elimination of the family's economic role. The business extended family can be observed mainly among the Christians, somewhat among the Druze, and seldom among the Moslems. This is due to the fact that the first two groups contained many landowners, some of whom converted their lands into new businesses..

Agricultural Extended Family. The agricultural extended family is comparable, to some extent, to that of the modest farmers in the agrarian period. However, several new elements can be observed as a result of the socioeconomic changes noted earlier. This extended family is based on agricultural work. The labor force is composed of the father, mother, unmarried daughters, children of school age, and one of the adult sons (usually the elder). The other adult sons work as wage laborers in nonagricultural jobs. They work on family lands only during their extra time. Some local labor is hired during the harvest seasons. While the son who works in agriculture remains with his parents after marriage, the other sons leave the extended household upon marriage. The father controls the family property, but each of the sons who work as wage laborers has his own account. The father has full authority over the family members, even those who reside apart. The division of the inheritance usually occurs after the father's death.

> Case 2. The family had several plots of land scattered around the settlement. Most of the farming was based on irrigation, with some dry farming and olive trees. The agricultural work was handled by the father, and the mother, their children-- two unmarried daughters and the elder son. One of the other three adult sons worked as a teacher, and the other two were laborers in the nearby industrial area. During the harvest season all the sons had a special 'vacation' in order to assist their family. The father received all the family income from agriculture. He controlled the land and the other property. Although the sons who worked outside had their own accounts, there was some cooperation among the family members. The elder son lived with the original household for seven years after his marriage. The second son moved to a separate residence in the same neighborhood immediately upon his marriage. This evoked a demand from the elder son's wife for independent residence. "I have the same right to be independent, to enjoy our life, and to have my privacy," she said. The problem was solved by building a separate apartment for the elder son in the same yard. Despite the separation in residence, the family members continued to maintain intensive relationships. The father played a crucial role in this sense. He said enthusiastically: "The most important aim in my life is to keep my children together and to reinforce their mutual commitment to each other. If I die, they can decide whether to continue in this way or not. I wish from the bottom of my heart that they will stay together. Id ala id bitn" (one hand strengthens the other).

The agricultural household is partially extended in terms of residence and in its role as a unit for production and consumption. The family members compose two familial units: extended and nuclear with tight linkages between them. This type can be found almost solely among the Druze, in particular among those who originated from large landowners. This can be traced to the fact

99

that, unlike the other religious groups, the Druze landowners have kept their lands intact and thus have kept the continuity of agricultural work.

The Extended Household of Residence. This type of extended household maintains the minimum characteristics of the extended family. There is no common economic base and the family does not function either as a production unit or as a consumption unit. It is extended only in terms of residence for a limited period of time in the life cycle.

> Case 3. The father was an unskilled worker. The two adult sons worked as wage laborers in Haifa. After the marriage of the elder son, the parents allocated a room for him in the same house. This served as a bedroom in which he put the wardrobe, the double bed, and some of his private things. The other facilities continued to be common for all the family members. "This was a difficult situation," noted the father, "but we could not support his (the son's) marriage, purchase land and to build a house at the same time, since our income is restricted." "I do not see anything wrong in living together," added the mother. "After all, we wanted all the family members to remain together." The daughter-in-law suffered most. She had to take part in all the housework. She was subject to control and criticism by all the family members, in particular by her mother-in-law. She said with embitterment, "my father was reluctant for my marriage because the bridegroom had no independent house. My father-in-law promised that within one year after the marriage we would be able to have our own house. My father eventually, agreed. Unfortunately I had to live with the family of my husband for five years before we moved apart. The life with my husband's family was intolerable. I had to serve all the family members and I had nothing to decide about, even my own things. My mother-in-law kept saying the new generation know nothing about life and they have to obey the old generation who have a deep experience in life. When I wanted to have some privacy with my husband, my father in-law accused us that we were not social. The situation was aggravated after the birth of our first child. Everyone in the family wanted to play 'the role of the wise,' to advise me how to treat the baby and to intervene in everything."

The household functioned for one year as a consumption unit. The members of the household had their meals together, but this situation caused continuous tension between the mother-in-law and her daughter-in-law, since the mother-in-law "demanded too much and intervened in everything." To ease some of this tension, the husband (son) thought it would be better to be separated even at the same house. Thus, the kitchen continued to be common but with two pots: one for the son's family and the second for the other members of the household.

The extended family in residence can be observed among all the religious groups. It is prominent in particular among the Moslems and the in-migrant groups. This type is similar to that found among the lowest stratum in the pre-1948 period where lack of resources created a compulsory extended household of family necessity. But unlike the agrarian period, this type does not even function as a labor unit. As a result, the father's authority is diminished, although it does not disappear. Its continuity is derived from the community social context, which emphasizes the need of keeping some sort of linkage and mutual commitments among the family members, and from the family necessity. Different needs (marriage, housing, etc.) cannot be accomplished without the joint effort of the family members, since most of these households belong to the lowest stratum with restricted resources.

In sum, our analysis of the characteristics and the roles of the extended family suggests several conclusions. Throughout the several time periods, there was no single, typical extended family structure, but rather a diversity of types, each of which had some elements in common with others as well as some unique elements. Therefore, discussing the extended family in general terms may be misleading. Our analysis emphasizes the need for a cautious definition of the extended family which takes into consideration the several elements of this familial unit. A clear distinction has to be made between structural and associative elements, as well as between the extended family which is the result of necessity and that which is of voluntary interest.

Our findings suggest that the modernization process affects the several types of the extended family in a diverse, rather than an overall, manner. While a rapid change has taken place in the structural elements, less changes were observed in the associative elements. The extended family structure is not the outcome of the cultural values or the ideological system, but is rather the result of economic constraints or economic and social convenience, depending on the type of extended family. Moreover, the several types are not determined by religious group. Religious affiliation affected family structure through the class division, in particular during the agrarian period. Each stratum was linked to a different familial type in almost all cases.

The extended family structure exerted a crucial influence on the nuclear family. The nuclear unit was submerged in the extended structure until a certain point in the life cycle, mainly after the father's death. This restricted the power of the young couples and eliminated their role in the family decision making.

What are the effects of the extended family structure on women's status and fertility patterns in Shefar-A'm? Is the marginality of the ideological system also consistent for women status and fertility? Does the modernization process affect these familial patterns in a similar way as the extended family? These questions will be addressed systematically in the next chapters.

5

Women's Status

The status of women has been researched extensively in the Middle East, relative to other issues of family life. Many of these studies have emphasized the centrality of values, norms, and belief systems as the major determinants of women's status. The focus has been on ideology rather than actual behavior, since the assumption was that ideology is the main determinant of women's status (see Al-Qazzaz, 1975; Van Dusen, 1976; Allman, 1978). Some researchers, who investigated issues of honor, shame, and women's modesty, were male investigators who obtained their information from male informants. Much less effort has been made to investigate the attitudes of women or their actual behavior (see Antoun, 1968; VanDusen, 1976; Shokeid, 1980).

Arab Middle Eastern women, in particular Moslem women, have been viewed as powerless, subservient, and submissive. Moslem culture has been treated as the major barrier to the improvements of women's status in terms of emancipation, educational and occupational attainments, and participation in the decision making process in the family and the broader community (see Allman, 1978). Antoun (1968:678) argued that "in the village, however, the ideology of women's inferiority finds its most intense expression neither in her legal nor ritual status, nor in beliefs about her rational capacity, but rather in views about her ethical capability. There is a firm belief that women are initiators in any illicit relations." Several studies have relied almost exclusively on expressions derived from folklore to verify the ideology of the inferiority of women in the Arab culture. Expressions such as "el-marah min dil er-ridjāl" (the woman is from the rib of the man) and "en-niswān ilhun nuss a qil" (women have but half a brain) are cited as illustrations of the weakness of women. Thus, a weak and cowardly man is dubbed "mitl el-marah" (like the woman) (Canaan, 1931:173).

Is it sufficient to study the status of women only through the prevailing ideology and belief system? Studies conducted in different places indicated a conspicuous gap between ideology and actual behavior. Even in a patriarchal society where family relations are dominated by husbands, wives may participate in many decisions (Ginat, 1975). A study conducted in a French peasant village concluded that while both sexes believe in the "myth" of male dominance in decision making, the important community and family decisions were made by women (Rogers, 1975).

These findings and others do not imply the need to abandon the analysis of the normative system derived from the cultural context of the community. They do, however, point to the need to adopt a broader approach combining the cultural context with other factors. In particular, there is a need to analyze the dynamics of the interaction between wives and husbands, between the spouses and the other family members, and between the family and the surrounding community.

In the analysis of changes of the status of women, two main theoretical approaches have been the most prominent: the modernization approach and the resources theory. Some scholars have merged both within one broader approach, but usually they have been formulated separately (see Lee and Petersen, 1983). Students of modernization posit that the increasing processes of modernization and westernization, the spread of mass media, and the exposure to agents of westernization lead to major change in the status of women. Traditional values and norms, which regulate the status of women in traditional society, are replaced by modern values. This process enhances the emancipation of women's activity at both the communal and the family levels. The exposure to western ideologies affects women by carrying the message of greater sexual equality (see Pat Caldwell, 1977). The modernization approach assumes a high correlation between developing modern attitudes and becoming modern. Therefore, changes in the normative base towards women lead to parallel changes in actual behavior (see Inkeles and Smith, 1974; Datan, 1972).

Some studies conducted in developing societies have noted an inverse impact of modernization and contact with agents of modernization on women's status. Shokeid (1980:191) noted that the interaction between Moslems and Jews in a mixed city in

104

Israel had an inverse effect on the first group by "bracing them in their traditional beliefs about the threat their womenfolk presented to their honor." Modernization of the economic structure was also noted as inversely related to women's status. Dealing with women's role in economic development, Boserup noted that "change from traditional to modern farming tends to enhance men's prestige at the expense of women by widening the gap in their levels of knowledge and training. In some cases, this tendency is further strengthened by the change in production patterns which give men the role of independent cultivators who make decisions while women's role is reduced to that of family aids or of hired workers on land belonging to male farmers, with a correspondingly enhanced male status over women" (Boserup, 1970:57). Similar conclusions were reached by Bossen (1975) in which he noted that a conspicuous decline in women's status was the result of modernization changes in the economic system, which decreased women's resources and increased their dependency on their husbands.

The later arguments can be connected with the resources theory, which was first suggested by Blood and Wolfe (1960). The resources theory posits that "with the marital relationship each spouse's decision making power varies directly with the amount and value of the resources which that spouse provides to the marriage or to the other spouse" (Lee and Petersen, 1983:23). Therefore, the marital partner with the greater personal resources relative to the other will also have greater relative power (see Blood and Wolfe, 1960; Elliott and Moskoff, 1983). Resources may be classified into two categories: socioeconomic (material) resources and personal skills or characteristics. Most studies have concentrated on socioeconomic resources which include education, occupational status, income, and employment prestige (see Katz and Peres, 1985; Lee and Petersen, 1983).

Students of the resources theory have reached different conclusions. Some have completely confirmed the theory (see Cromwell and Olson, 1975). Others have found it applicable to modern societies but not to patriarchal societies, where the unequivocal normative system minimizes the effect of resources on wife-husband power within the family (Rodman, 1972). It has also been argued that the possession of resources affects women's power but not husband's. Moreover, some vital resources (education) have been negatively associated with husband's power (see Fox, 1973; Katz and Peres, 1985).

As mentioned before, our study does not aim to test a specific theoretical approach, but rather uses these approaches as a way

of facilitating our understanding of family life styles. The status
of women among the several groups in Shefar-A'm will be
examined for different periods and under different economic
systems. The effect of modernization and the resources of the
family will be analyzed along with the socio-cultural context and
the changing modes of production in the community. Throughout
our analysis, a clear distinction will be made between women's
status at the family level, as reflected in power for women and
their participation in family decision making, and at the
community level and as reflected in the educational attainments of
women, their participation in the nondomestic labor force and in
social and political activities. In addition, the normative level and
the actual behavior will be treated separately. Our major
questions are: What is the nature of women's status throughout
the several periods within the family and the community? What
are the determinants of women's status--the normative-ideological
system, modernization factors, distribution of resources within the
family, or a combination of different factors?

Ideological System

The ideological system which emphasizes the inferiority of
women and the subordination of wives to their husbands may be
observed in Shefar-A'm, in particular during the agrarian period.
Mothers prepared their daughters before marriage to obey their
husbands and the other family members and to behave only
according to their will. "Sāhat el-im el-hanūn ùqalt ya waladi,
kūni mutia laibn el-bet wil-waladi" the mother said on the day of
her daughter's marriage (Oh, my daughter, be obedient to the
family [husband's family] and the children). Several expressions
reflected the superiority of males over females: "Tikbar haiyeh
wala tdjib bnaiyeh" (May she grow and be a snake and not give
birth to a girl) and "el-marah mermerah" (the woman causes the
bitter life). The birth of a boy was perceived as "building a
house," assuring the continuity of the family name, and as a sign
of the family happiness. The birth of girl was treated with
disdain, since "houses full of girls are houses in ruin" (dūr el-banāt
kharabat). (See also Granqvist, 1935). In contrast to these
expressions, we found other expressions which emphasized the
importance of women's role in educating children, in particular the
daughters, and in managing the budget of the family: "El-marah
el-asile bitdjeeb asile" (the noble woman gives birth to a noble
daughter) and "el-zalami janna wil-marah bannah" (the man

106

earns the money and the woman builds the house).

The ideology of the superiority of men over women and the image of the wife as a subordinate are still observed in the community, despite the socio-cultural changes noted earlier. Systematic participant observation and a large number of informal conversations revealed that this ideology is deeply rooted, so much so that a person who is perceived by the community as weak at home tries to find several apologetic words to justify the "unique" relationship with his wife, such as "tfahum" (mutual understanding) or "ittifaq" (agreement), etc. Or he tries on every occasion to stress that he, not his wife, is the dominant person.

The perception of male dominance is shared as well by wives. But they tend to emphasize the power of husbands much less than it is perceived by husbands themselves. This was reflected in the answers of the respondents to the question: Who should have the final say in the family? Of the responses, 82 percent of the husbands compared to 62 percent of the wives noted the husband; 18 percent of the husbands compared to 38 percent of the wives noted that every decision should be a joint one of both spouses. In contrast to the high agreement between husbands and wives on the ideology, there is less agreement on actual behavior. This was reflected in the respondents' answers to the question: When you have disagreement on a specific issue who has the final say? Overall, husbands tended to indicate the dominance of husbands in the family decision making (Table 5.1). The extent of the perception of the husband's dominance is asymmetric: 78 percent of the husbands compared to only 33 percent of the wives reported the husband's dominance, whether by indicating that he has the final say or by indicating that they had not faced such a situation.

The agreement between husband and wife is usually perceived as the outcome of the husband's dominance. A considerable number of respondents, in particular men, noted that it is disgraceful to have disagreement between spouses or not to reach a decision. Most of the wives (60 percent), but only a small minority of the husbands (22 percent), reported that the husband does not have the final say and that the disagreement is resolved by the intervention of a third person (relative, friend, etc.). Nevertheless, it is clear that dominance by women is unacceptable; only seven percent of the wives and none of the husbands reported that wives have the final say.

Does the gap between ideology and the perceived actual situation indicate higher women's status than that reflected in the normative system? Our findings answer this question affirmatively. Women are not as marginal as they are described

TABLE 5.1

FAMILY DECISION-MAKING AS PERCEIVED BY
HUSBANDS AND WIVES, SHEFAR-A'M, 1982

Who Has the Final Say	Husband	Wife	Total
Husband	40.0	18.0	29.2
Wife	0.0	7.0	3.1
A relative intervenes	10.0	20.0	14.4
Another person intervenes (neighbor, friend, etc.)	7.0	10.0	8.3
No final decision is reached	5.0	30.0	16.0
Have not faced such situation	38.0	15.0	29.0
Total	100.0	100.0	100.0
N	120	120	240

by the normative system. The dominance of the husband does not imply the marginality of women. The emphasis of the husband's dominance, whether by him or by his wife, is aimed mainly to enhance his position in the community. At home, women played an important role in the several fields of decision making. As Ginat noted, "The Arab ideology of the women's inferior status has a marked impact on her conduct. There is a tendency for her to underplay such influence as she has and to exert it as far as possible without drawing attention to herself and to her influence. By behaving in this manner, she actually allows the male in the family to play the role of the dominant head without herself losing any of her influence. There are two mechanisms at work--one aimed to reducing tensions, while the other operates to forestall tension and conflict" (Ginat, 1975:333).

Our findings revealed that women are involved in the decision making at the family level: 70 percent of the husbands and 85 percent of the wives reported that wives had an active role in the decision about building a new house and purchasing furniture; 65 percent of the husbands and 72 percent of the wives reported that family visits are the outcome of a joint husband-wife decision. This situation emerges as well in family budgeting. Only 13 percent of the husbands solely control the family budget. In 79 percent of the households, women have access to the family budget in some way. Only in 8 percent of the households is the budget controlled by the husband's parents. These are chiefly agricultural or business extended households, in which the patriarch father controls the family property including the budget (see chapter 4).

Women's part in making financial decisions is not uniform. It depends on the kind of activity. While women are very active in purchasing food and clothing, they are less prominent in activities which involve contact with public institutions (Table 5.2). Although the vast majority of the wage earners are men, women play a decisive role in managing the family budget and in affecting priorities of what to purchase and how much to spend. Among families of the lower stratum, the husband usually gives his wife the entire wage and says, "khudi el-maā sh wil masūliyyeh" (take the wage and the responsibility). Women who belong to this stratum are known as "mdebrāt" (frugal).

The marginal role of women in contacts with public institutions can be traced to their marginal role at the community level, as will be discussed subsequently. Men are more embedded in bureaucratic affairs because they have frequent contact with the broader society, and they are usually more educated than

TABLE 5.2

WOMEN'S ROLE IN THE FAMILY FINANCIAL DEALINGS,
SHEFAR-A'M, 1982

Kind of Activity	Activity Performer				
	Husband	Wife	Husband and Wife	Extended Family Members	Total
Purchasing clothing and other needs for children	8.0	38.0	42.0	12.0	100.0
Purchasing foodstuffs	30.0	53.0	17.0	0.0	100.0
Payment of telephone, water, and electricity accounts	67.0	20.0	10.0	3.0	100.0
Payment for children's schooling expenditures	60.0	23.0	17.0	0.0	100.0
Conducting bank account	78.0	13.0	9.0	0.0	100.0

N = 240

women. Moreover, a considerable proportion of men are not willing to expose their wives to strangers, particularly males, since most of the people who work in public institutions are men. Analyzing the religious groups, there were no differences between them in terms of women's involvement in purchasing clothing and food. A significant difference among the religious groups emerged in terms of contact with public institutions. The percentage of women who handled the family account with public institutions was 40 percent among Christians, 15 percent among Moslems, and only 9 percent among Druze. This is because Christian women are more educated and more involved in the community than women from other religious groups. However, during the last decade these differences have narrowed.

There is a glaring gap between women's status in the family and at the community level. While women have a relatively high status at home, their role in the community is more limited. In the mid -1980s, only 11 percent of women work outside the home. Among the 650 women who participate in the labor force in Shefar-A'm, 128 work in teaching or in clerical jobs, 190 in industry, and 332 in other unskilled jobs. One of the major obstacles to the participation of women in the labor force is the disappearance of the local economic base and the absence of substantial resources within the community, in particular industry. There is a readiness among large segments of men to approve women's work outside the home: 45 percent of the men fully approve, 25 percent partially approve, and 30 percent oppose women working outside the home. Most of those who partially approve or oppose women working noted that they would be less reluctant if the place of work were within the community.

Our findings support the conclusion noted in other developing societies regarding the negative effect of modernization on women's productivity (see Boserup, 1970; Bossen, 1975). The drastic occupational changes which occurred after the establishment of Israel resulted, among other things, in the relative decline in women's labor productivity. Under the agrarian economy most women took an active part in the labor force. Among the large and the modest landowners, they worked in the family fields, and among the small landowners or the landless, they worked as agricultural wage laborers. Some documents indicated that several Christian women were landowners. They were involved in land purchase and sale and had complete control over their property. The massive land confiscation after the establishment of Israel and the lack of other substantial resources have also decreased drastically women's ownership of any kind of property.

The weakness of women's status in the community is reflected as well in their low involvement in social and political activities. Only 8 percent of the women compared to 21 percent of the men are members of local organizations; 6 percent of the women compared to 20 percent of the men are members of national organizations; and only 3 percent of the women compared to 14 percent of the men are members of a political party. Political activity is still considered the men's exclusive field, whether at the local level or at the national level. Since the establishment of the Shefar-A'm municipality in 1910, there has been no female candidate in the municipal elections. Women's political activity at the national level is observed in particular among those affiliated with the communist party. They are organized in three main groups: "abnā el-kadiheen" (children of the proletariat) for ages 10-14; "shabibat el-hizb" (youths of the communist party) for ages 15-18; and "el-nisā el-dimuqrāṭiyyat" (the democratic women) for ages 19 and over. However, even in the communist party there is a small proportion of active women compared to men. The secretary of the communist youths indicated that only about 11 percent of the party's active members are women.

There is a clear relationship between the activity of women and the life cycle. A major decline in women's activity may be observed after marriage. Those who continue to be active are influenced mostly by their husbands. Almost all women have the same political affiliation as their husbands. A wife is expected to follow the vote of her husband. If she does not, he will be viewed as a weak person, because he has no authority even over his wife's vote (bimunish ala ṣot maratoh).

That women are less interested in political affairs than men was reflected in the answers to the question: How often do you talk about political issues? Of the respondents, 22 percent of the wives compared to 68 percent of the husbands reported frequently; 55 percent of the wives compared to 4 percent of the husbands noted rarely. It is not clear whether women do not discuss political issues because of a lack of awareness or a lack of interest. In relation to this, however, some husbands and wives noted frequent conflict between them because of the programs they wish to watch on television. Men tend to watch news, political panels, and sports, while women tend to watch movies or other entertainment programs.

Education is the most prominent field in which women have achieved tremendous progress at the communal level. In 1952, there were four elementary schools with a total of 790 pupils in Shefar-A'm. Females constituted one-third of the pupils. A conspicuous religious gap existed. Christians constituted 80 percent of the female students compared to about 12 percent for Moslems and 8 percent for Druze. In the secondary school, females constituted a negligible proportion of the total (about 10 percent), all of them Christians. Comparison with the 1980s indicates a very sharp increase. Females constitute about 50 percent of the pupils at both the elementary and secondary levels. The disappearance of sex difference in terms of formal education was accompanied by parallel disappearance of the gap among the several religious groups. There is a high proportion of literate women aged 18 and over: 90 percent among Christians, 80 percent among local Moslems, 79 percent among refugee Moslems, and 75 percent among Druze.

Modes of Production and Control of Resources

It is difficult to clearly identify and measure the several personal and material resources which may affect women's status (see Lee and Petersen, 1983). For example, it is most difficult to measure quantitatively the different support which a woman may receive from her paternal family after marriage. The elimination of this support also eliminates one of the important resources for married women in Arab society (see Rosenfeld, 1960; Ginat, 1975; Patai, 1983; Antoun, 1968). Moreover, it is difficult to quantify the resources of spouses in the extended family, since the husband as well as the wife are completely dependent on the patriarch father, who controls the family resources. In considering the measurement of these resources, we will emphasize the dynamics of the interaction between wives and husbands, between the spouses and the other family members, and between the family and the surrounding community.

During the agrarian period, the amount of power of women and their level of participation in family decision making were linked to the different types of extended family, rather than with the possession of material resources. A woman's power was the outcome of her relations with the three dependency centers: the husband, the husband's family, and her own paternal family. Several contradictory norms were developed in the community and affected women's status in diverse ways.

Among merchants and large landowners, women played an important role in the several aspects of family life. Evidence from diaries of Christians who were large landowners during the Mandatory Period showed, for example, that the husband mentioned his wife's active assistance in making several decisions regarding the family's properties and the marriage of their sons. On March 3, 1941 he wrote:

> I and my wife went to see the land which we we are going to purchase....we decided not to buy this land, since it is far from our lands and close to the Bedouin settlement.

On May 22, 1943 he included:

> My wife registered the crops on the threshing floor. We discussed its division: some for the workers, some for our consumption, and the rest for sale.

The diary also reported about the process of the son's marriage and clearly revealed the wife's role in the selection of the brides, the decision about the marriage ceremony, and the son's residence after marriage. In this stratum, women had a strong status at home, although the family lands were registered in the husband's name and the wife had relatively negligible economic activity, since all the work was handled by hired labor or on the basis of crop-sharing. In addition, women from the highest stratum never worked outside the family.

The high status of women was also observed among Druze landowners. Informants reported that women in this stratum strongly affected the family affairs. We have evidence about a man who was compelled to call off the sale of some plots of land because of the reluctance of his wife. Some women even affected indirectly the community political affairs. Several informants noted the case of one of the Druze community leaders who consulted with his wife about all the community affairs in which he was involved, although his wife was never seen in public.

Similar patterns were found among Moslems. The fact that there were few families among Moslems who belonged to the large landowners made the women's status in this stratum more prominent. This evoked the envy of women who belonged to lower strata. One of the female informants who belonged to a landless family noted:

> "When I compared my life with our wealthy neighbor (who belonged to the large landowners) I felt deeply oppressed. While I worked hard, she enjoyed her life. She almost

never worked in the family fields. But she received everything she wanted."

A prominent example of a strong woman in the high stratum, which is still remembered by old people in Shefar-A'm, is Fulleh Hamādi, the Mother of Muhammad Hamādi, the Mukhtar of the Moslems during the Mandatory Period. She affected Moslem community affairs through her son. When the relations between Moslems and Christians deteriorated after the murder of one Moslem by a Christian, hundreds of Moslems from the surrounding villages came to take revenge. Fulleh Hamādi prevented bloodshed. She said to her son "ashi wmashi" (after dinner send them back [to their villages]).

Our findings support the argument that high status among women may be found in the higher stratum. In contrast to some researchers (see Katz and Peres, 1985), we suggest that this phenomenon is not restricted to modern societies. It may also be observed in agrarian societies.

The status of women was completely different among the extended households of the modest and the small peasants and the landless. The lack of economic resources and the relative long duration of residence with the extended household restricted the married son and hindered his efforts to establish an independent family. The weakness of the young wife was not because of her subordination to her husband, but rather because of the dependency of both the spouses on the extended family system. The husband lacked any authority, since this was concentrated on the hands of the patriarch father. Therefore, the woman's status was the outcome of her relations with all the family members: the husband and the husband's father, brothers, mother (see also Rosenfeld, 1960; Lutfiyya, 1970). We have several cases to exemplify this fact. An old women (72 years at the time) noted:

> My life with my husband's family was very difficult. I cannot forget one day when my father-in-law entered my room and started to curse me, he even beat me without saying why. I realized later that this was because I refused the request of my mother-in-law to work in the family fields. Because in that day I had to take care of my sick child."

Another woman (69 years at the time) noted:

> I lived with my husband's family for eleven years after

115

marriage. I never felt that I am married to one husband,. since every one of the family members tried his authority on me. Even my married sister-in-law intervened in everything. She kept criticizing me. My mother-in-law was the most cruel. She placed her authority on me, even much more than my husband did."

Women in this stratum had a double burden. They worked in the family fields or as wage laborers and handled the several household tasks. The younger daughter-in-law suffered the most, since she had to take care of all the family members in addition to her husband and children. Women were very active economically but they never benefited from their work since it was submerged in the extended family properties.

However, even in this stratum women's status differed according to the several stages in the life cycle. A woman's status as a young wife in the extended family differed completely from her status as a wife in her own household and later as a mother-in-law in the recreated extended household. For the bride, the most restrictive relationship was that conducted with the mother-in-law. The bride is expected to obey her mother-in-law. The husband is expected to support his mother against his wife or at least to be neutral. The mother-in-law who suffered in a dependency relationship in the early stages of her marriage repeats the same experience with her daughter-in-law. The transition from weakness to strength is fully exploited by the mother-in-law who places her authority on the family members, especially on her sons and their wives. In Shefar-A'm we found the same proverbs reported by Granquist (1935:147) in a Palestinian village regarding bride/mother -in-law relationships:

in kan il-bahr bisir jinne
umr il-hama ma habbat il-kinne
in kan il-bahr bisir miqta
umr il-kinne mā habbat il-hamma.

(Even if the sea were a paradise
the mother-in-law could never love the daughter-in-law
and even if the sea were a field of watermelon
the daughter-in-law would never love the mother-in-law.)

The rules of inheritance and the property system affected the status of women in the agrarian society. Land was the main economic base as well as a symbol for social status (see Rosenfeld,

1964; Granquist, 1935). Among the religious groups in Shefar-A'm, there were only a few Christian women who took their part in the inheritance. Among Moslems and Druze, almost all women deferred their right to their brothers. This is despite the fact that Islamic religious rules have secured their portion. According to the Qurān, a woman has the right to inherit one-half of the man's share. The property system was solely controlled by men, however, and women were completely dependent. This reinforced the men's status at the expense of the women.

However, several social rules were observed among the religious groups which were aimed at supporting the status of women and compensating them for the loss of property. The Druze women benefited from applying the Druze religious rules which secured their rights within the family in different ways (see Layish, 1977). According to these rules, every mature man had to write a detailed testament regarding the property division and the other family affairs. Analysis of the available testaments revealed that women rights were mentioned explicitly. For instance, in one of these testaments dated December 12, 1945, the father registered his lands in the name of his two sons. This was conditioned by their fulfillment of detailed points regarding the rights of the unmarried sisters. Among other things, the sons were committed to safeguard all the needs of their sisters: to sustain them, not to ask them to do any work in the fields, and to give them free access to the crops or to any of the family properties.

The other religious groups adopted similar norms to support women. The most prominent is the continuity of the strong relationship and commitment between a woman and her paternal family after marriage. This has two main beneficial effects for the married woman. A woman is considered an integral part of her paternal family honor throughout her life. She retains her father's name, who continues to have full responsibility for any deficiency in her behavior. During the early years of marriage a woman "who is considered something of an outsider by her husband's family, can always count on aid and sympathy of her own father and brothers. The very knowledge that these men are lined up solidly behind her, and are ready, if need be, even to fight for her, puts a restraint on her husband's family in their treatment of a young daughter-in-law" (Patai, 1983:119-120). In addition, the continuous commitment of the paternal family to their daughter after marriage is translated into material awards. Brothers know that they have to compensate their sister for her share in the property. A woman receives from her father and

117

brothers valuable gifts in every feast "ideyyeh" and every occasion "hadeyyeh." These are considered as their elementary duty "wājib" (see Rosenfeld, 1960:68).

The commitment of the paternal family to the daughter after marriage, which originated in the agrarian period, continues to be observed also at present. This despite the drastic economic transformation and the various sociocultural changes in the community. In-depth interviews, systematic participant observation, and conversations with informants revealed that parents support their daughter in different ways before and after marriage. They take the responsibility for a considerable part of the marriage expenses in furnishing the new house. While the changes in the economic structure from peasantry to wage labor has decreased drastically women's productivity, the support they receive from the paternal family has increased. The bride price, which was given to the father by the groom to compensate him for his loss of the daughter's labor force (see Granquist, 1935), has been replaced by different things the groom is committed to give the bride in order to secure her future. Unlike the agrarian period, the daughter's marriage does not imply economic loss. The drastic decrease in agriculture and the small proportion of women in the labor force have reduced the economic contribution of women to the family income. Therefore, during the marriage negotiations, the father usually says to the groom "eksi ukhud" (just purchase the bride her needs [clothing and other personal needs] and marry her). The only condition required from the groom is usually to build a separate house far from his family. This could not be done under the agrarian system since the nuclear family was submerged in the extended household. Any investment in the daughter's house after marriage would have added to the property of the patriarch father and not to the young spouses (see Rosenfeld, 1980).

Male children constitute an important part of the wife's resources, especially when they reach maturity. They support their mother in her relationship with the father and later with their wives (see Patai, 1983). We identified a number of cases in which the father was prevented from marrying another wife by his adult sons in order to protect their mother's status. As noted by other studies (Patai, 1983; Rosenfeld, 1960), women without male children have lower status. The husband may marry another wife hoping to have male children. After the death of the husband, a wife without male children has to return to her father's house, since she has no right of inheritance. Only sons could grant her this right.

Under the agrarian system, the economic productivity of women per se had almost no effect on their status within the family or within the community. Is this lack of a relationship between women's status and their participation in the labor force restricted to the agrarian period? It may be argued that women's economic productivity had no major effect under the agrarian system because women worked mostly as domestic laborers, rather than as independent wage earners. In the modern phase, participation in the labor force, reinforced by other socioeconomic resources (education, prestige, etc.), is expected to exert a major effect on women's status (see Blood and Wolfe, 1960; Rodman, 1972; Fox, 1973; Lee and Petersen, 1983; Katz and Peres, 1985). We examined this point by in-depth interviews and participant observation. Four main items reflecting decision making at the family level were selected: family visits, building a house, budget control, and purchases. The first two reflect occasional decisions, while the latter two reflect day-to-day affairs. Each item was divided into three categories: the first reflects a high participation of the wife in the decision making, the second moderate, and the third weak participation. The first category was assigned 2 points, the second 1 point, and the third 0. All the items were aggregated, and women's status was ranked according to this order:

0-2 points	weak status
3 points	modest status
6-8 points	strong status

Socioeconomic resources were measured by occupation and education.

Overall, the findings indicate no relationship between women's participation in the labor force and their status in the family. Women's work per se has no major effect on the power of women and their participation in decision making (Table 5.3). Nevertheless, women's work strongly affects their self image. A strong relationship was found between participation in the labor force and women's perception of who has the final say in the family. Of the working women, 31 percent reported that they have the final say when there is a controversial issue concerning family affairs and only 17 percent reported that their husbands

TABLE 5.3

WOMEN'S STATUS IN THE FAMILY AND THE COMMUNITY BY
OCCUPATION AND EDUCATION, SHEFAR-A'M, 1982

Socioeconomic Factors	In the Family				In the Community Members in Local Organizations
	Weak	Modest	Strong	Total	
Occupation					
Not Employed	25.5	39.5	35.0	100.0	6.0
Employed	28.5	34.2	37.3	100.0	13.5
Education					
No Education	30.0	37.1	32.9	100.0	4.0
Primary Education	27.0	42.5	30.5	100.0	5.2
Higher Education	11.0	26.5	62.5	100.0	15.0
Total	26.6	37.4	36.0	100.0	8.0
N = 120					

have the final say. Among the nonworking women, the percentages were 3 and 29, respectively. Therefore, the gap between the actual situation and the perceived status was greater among working than among nonworking women. This in itself generates conflict between husbands and wives. The more the gap between the expected and the real situation, the greater the conflict (see Merton, 1968). This point clearly emerged in the open interviews. One interviewee noted:

> The relations with my wife continued in the right way until my wife started to work. On almost every occasion when we discussed anything she said that she has nothing to be indebted to me, since she can sustain herself and she does not need me or anybody to secure her needs.

Another interviewee noted:

> When I chose my wife I thought that she would be of great help since she worked with me in the same factory. But unfortunately after our marriage I realized that I miscalculated. The problems started soon after the marriage. My wife argued all the time that she contributes to the household exactly as I do, and thus she has the right to take any decision which seems to be appropriate in her eyes, even if I disagree. I was strongly disappointed. This situation lasted about one year even after we had our first child. I felt that we cannot continue to live together. We were separated for a couple of months. Within this period we met several times. Finally she agreed to return home after she left work. Today our life is completely different. We are happily married.

The wife said:

> When I worked the same as my husband and I almost earned the same wage, I felt that I have no reason to be subordinated to him. I have exactly the same right to be independent. When we were separated I was convinced that somewhere I was mistaken. I appreciated my husband's decision to leave his job in the factory and to be self-employed in order to suffice all the family needs.

It should not be inferred that the wife's working is necessarily accompanied by a conflict relationship with her husband, or that nonparticipation of a woman in the labor force is an assurance of good relations between spouses. Nevertheless, we suggest that working women have a greater potential for conflict with their husbands than nonworking women.

While a woman's occupation has no effect on her status at the family level, it has a major effect at the community level. Working women, much more so than housewives, are active socially and politically through their membership in voluntary organizations, political parties, and, of course, professional organizations (Table 5.3).

The effect of education on women's status differs according to the educational level. While almost no relationship is observed between women's education and participation in the family decision making at the level of no or primary education, there is a strong relationship at higher levels of education (see Table 5.3). The positive effect of higher education on women's status has been reported by several studies (see Katz and Peres, 1985). Women with higher education are from families who support a higher women's status, already reflected in the fact that they permitted the women to obtain a higher level of education. In addition, women at this level of education have a higher prestige than other women in the community because of the relative low percentage of women with a higher education, in particular among Moslems and Druze. Most of the women who are active in the community, socially or politically, are working women who have a higher education (see Table 5.3).

Modernization Factors

Our findings suggest no relationship between individual modernization factors (exposure to mass media, psychological modernization, and contact with Jews) and women's status, in particular at the behavioral level. Individual modernization factors do not distinguish between different types of women's status. Most surprising is the lack of relationship between women's status and contact with the Jewish population. Since Jews in Israel constitute the agents of westernization for Arabs, they are expected to transfer western values, which would reinforce women's status (see Kanaana, 1975; Avitsour, 1978).

To further examine the influence of the Jewish population, respondents were asked to point to their reference group in various fields: the relationship between husbands and wives, parents and children, males and females, family planning and socioeconomic achievements. For each field, respondents were asked to chose one of the following groups as their reference group: Jews in Israel, the Arab minority in Israel, Arab societies in the Middle East, Palestinians in the West Bank and Gaza, and groups within the community (other religious groups, neighbors, friends, relatives, etc.). Overall, the findings revealed that the Jewish population is a marginal reference group regarding family lifestyles, but it is the main reference group regarding socioeconomic achievements. In contrast to the modernization approach which assumes that the traditional or less modern sector perceives the modern sector as the major reference group, our findings suggest that the individual or the group has several reference groups at the same time and at various levels. Married persons in Shefar-A'm tend to evaluate the relationships within the family with other groups in the local community with whom daily, informal relationships take place (this point will be discussed in the next chapter).

The perception of the Jewish population as the main reference group in terms of socioeconomic achievements is due to fact that the local community as well as the Arabs in Israel are completely dependent economically and politically on the Jewish sector. The Jewish dominant sector has control over the economic opportunity structure and the educational system of the Arabs in Israel as a whole (see Smooha, 1980; Mari, 1978). Therefore, the extent of the socioeconomic achievements of Arabs is mainly evaluated by comparison with the Jewish sector.

Does contact with the Jewish population in Israel have an indirect negative effect on women's status, in the sense that men are reinforced in their traditional beliefs about women? Shokeid (1980) suggests that when such a pattern exists, it is due to men's fear of the expected negative effect of western values on the sacred values of family honor and women''s modesty. Respondents were asked to evaluate the effect of contact with Jews on women's status (Table 5.4). Overall, the data show that husbands as well as wives perceive that contact with the Jewish population has no effect on women's status. Wives, more than husbands, tended to emphasize the positive and de-emphasize the negative effects of contact with the Jewish population. Among husbands, 53 percent reported no effect, 22 percent reported a positive effect, and 25 percent reported a negative effect. Among wives, the percentages were 51, 45, and 4 percent, respectively. While no considerable differences in the perception of wives were observed among the religious groups, large differences were observed in the perception of husbands. Contact with the Jewish

TABLE 5.4

THE PERCEIVED EFFECT OF THE CONTACT WITH THE JEWISH
POPULATION ON WOMEN, BY RELIGIOUS GROUP,
SHEFAR-A'M, 1982

Religious Groups by Spouse	No Effect	Perceived Effect Positive Effect	Negative Effect	Total
Moslems				
Husbands	35.0	18.0	47.0	100.0
Wives	53.0	41.0	6.0	100.0
Christians				
Husbands	65.0	17.0	18.0	100.0
Wives	48.0	48.0	4.0	100.0
Druze				
Husbands	49.0	36.0	15.0	100.0
Wives	51.0	46.0	3.0	100.0
Total				
Husbands	53.0	22.0	25.0	100.0
Wives	51.0	45.0	4.0	100.0

N = 240

population tends to be evaluated as: negative among Moslems, neutral among Christians, and positive among Druze. The greatest gap between the attitudes of husbands and wives was observed among Moslems.

Detailed conversations revealed that respondents who emphasized the positive effect of contact with the Jews perceived that this contact has brought about women's education and other socioeconomic aspirations. Those who emphasized the negative effect perceived that this contact exposed women to a different culture, whose values contradicted their values of women's modesty and family honor. Men, more than women, feel threatened by this contact, since they are considered responsible for protecting women and the family honor (see Antoun, 1968). The tendency of Druze to emphasize the positive impact of the Jewish population may be traced to the fact that Druze are more Israeli oriented. As noted earlier, the process of religious particularism, which was introduced by the Israeli government after the establishment of Israel, was most successful among the Druze community.

Our findings partially support Shokeid's conclusion (1980) that a potential negative effect from contact with the Jewish population on the status of women has to be taken into consideration. We suggest further that contact with the Jewish population is generally perceived to have no effect on the status of women. In addition, we suggest there is a need to emphasize the diverse, rather than the overall, perception. This diversity is reflected in the differences between men and women and among religious groups. Moreover, we suggest that an in-depth examination of women's status has to take into consideration the attitudes and the actual behavior of both men and women and cannot be restricted only to male respondents.

Some of our findings do not support the modernization approach, and in fact some of them indicate a completely different conclusion than that hypothesized by this approach. Women's status at the community level (in terms of education and work outside the home) was encouraged mainly by noneducated parents aged 40 years and over. Educated young parents were not the innovators of such change. This was prominent in particular among the Druze community, in which women's status in the community was the lowest. Only during the 1970s did Druze women start to work outside the home and begin to obtain higher levels of education. At present, there are 168 Druze women working in several occupational branches, 26 girls at the high school, and 6 girls completing their higher education. The Druze religious leadership still exerts a major influence on the community and is most reluctant to accept this change. The parents who challenged this resistance and guided the change are not the elite of the community, but the group defined by the Druze as "marginal families." This generated the perception that they had nothing to lose by the criticism of their counterparts. Some of the innovators called themselves "the victims", since they absorbed all the criticism of the community and furnished the base for others to follow. At present, the participation of the Druze women in the community has become more widespread.

In sum, our analysis suggests the need to examine women's status at the family and the community levels in the framework of a broader approach which takes into consideration the dynamics of the interaction among family members and between the family and the surrounding community. It is of major importance to define women's resources within a wider view which includes direct socioeconomic resources as well as indirect social resources supported by the paternal family and the community context.

Modernization factors were found to have a negligible effect on women's status. Some of our findings even contradicted the family hypothesis. The assumption that family changes are an inevitable result of modernization may be misleading. Moreover, modern innovations are not necessarily led by the modern elite of the community. Under certain social and economic conditions, the innovators may be the group which is defined as traditional and marginal.

Religious affiliation is not a direct, powerful differentiator of women's status. Religious affiliation may affect women status through social class and family type. A glaring gap is observed between ideology and the actual behavior. The assumption that ideology and values reflect the actual situation may be distorting.

The effect of the extended family on women's status is not uniform. It depends on family type, social class, and stage in the life cycle. Among the upper class, women are accorded a higher status, while among extended families who belong to the modest or lower strata, women suffer the most. These differences are observed in particular during the early period after marriage. At the advanced stages of the life cycle, differences in women's status among the several strata narrow conspicuously.

To what extent can we build on these findings for our analysis of fertility patterns? Do religious affiliation, socioeconomic characteristics, ideological systems, and modernization factors affect fertility patterns in the same direction observed in women's status? How do the status of women and changes in the role of women affect their fertility? These issues form the basis of the following chapter.

6

Fertility and
Family Planning[1]

Recent data from the World Fertility Survey show that Arabs in eight Arab countries maintain relatively high levels of fertility. Total fertility rates range from 5.27 in Egypt to 8.51 in Yemen Arab Republic. Pro-natalist attitudes are evident among both older and younger women (Farid, 1984). A similar picture is observed among the Arab population in Israel. As noted in Chapter 2, Arabs in Israel, as well as in Shefar-A'm, experienced high fertility in the 1950s, which accelerated in the mid-1960s and began to decline significantly only in the 1970s. However, fertility patterns are not uniform among Arabs. Conspicuous differences are observed among the religious groups. The ordering of these groups from high to low fertility throughout the several periods is: Moslems, Druze, and Christians (see also Friedlander and Goldscheider, 1984).

The question may be raised: How can these differentials among the several groups be explained? There are two possible

----

1

Our data about family planning and fertility are based on interviews with women, unless noted otherwise. The data refer to the period after the establishment of Israel. No official statistics were available to cover fertility in the pre-1948 period. In addition, it was difficult to obtain reliable retrospective data about family planning by interviews (see also Eisenbach, 1978).

directions: The first is connected with the supply side of contraceptive use and the second with the demand side of fertility and orientation towards contraception (see Murty and Devos, 1984:223). The `family planning hypothesis is based on the supply side explanation. It posits that differentials in fertility and family planning among the several groups are a function of differential knowledge and access to contraception and family planning services (Murty and Devos, 1984:223). The two most prevailing hypotheses which focus on the demand side of the explanation are the characteristics hypothesis and minority group hypothesis. The characteristics hypothesis attributes fertility differentials to dissimilarities among groups in socioeconomic characteristics. When such differences disappear or are controlled statistically, differences in fertility should be eliminated, or at least converge to the point of insignificance (Goldscheider and Uhlenberg, 1969).

In contrast to the characteristics hypothesis, the minority status hypothesis postulates that even when minority-majority groups are similar socially, demographically, and economically, differences in fertility should continue to be observed. Minority group status, defined in terms of insecurity, marginality, and lack of integration, is hypothesized to have an independent effect on fertility. Differences in fertility within the minority group are expected according to the quality of minority group integration in the majority. Real or perceived opportunity for social mobility may substitute for equivalent social characteristics. Thus, achievement values must be present for minority group members to translate the "goals" of social mobility and concomitant acculturation for themselves and their children into the "means" which include family size limitation (Goldscheider and Uhlenberg, 1969:371). At higher socioeconomic levels, minority status interacts with socioeconomic status to reduce the fertility of the minority, even below majority levels (Goldscheider and Uhlenberg, 1969).

In studying a developing society, we may ask: Are fertility differentials among the several groups the outcome of differences in modernization levels? Caldwell, in a series of articles, has suggested an answer to this question. He has argued that "westernization" is a major factor in the demographic transition. He suggested that both family planning and a reduced family size emerge in developing societies in connection with the adoption of western culture. Westernization occurs due to the mass infusion of the mass media and mass education, and through contact with agents of westernization (Caldwell, 1976; 1977; 1982).

130

Westernization brings about fertility decline through the emotional nucleation of the family, whereby parents spend increasingly on their children while demanding--and receiving very little back in return (Caldwell, 1977). In this sense, the existence of strong kinship relationships and an extended family structure hinder family nucleation and the transition to a small family size (Caldwell, 1982). According to the westernization hypothesis, fertility differentials between various groups are related to different levels of westernization and family nucleation.

In this chapter, the family planning, the characteristics, the minority status, and the westernization hypotheses are employed to investigate differentials in fertility and family planning among the several groups in Shefar-A'm. While most of the previous studies have been restricted to the analysis of fertility rates, differentials in contraceptive behavior, and family planning have not been emphasized (see Murty and Devos, 1984). Our study considers fertility rates and family size and includes family planning through a separate analysis of contraceptive behavior and attitudes (normative level). It was difficult to obtain accurate data about the degree of actual family planning by direct questions. Therefore, a series of indirect questions were employed: number of children ever born, number of surviving children, birth spacing (we also used the identification card of women, where the accurate birth dates of children were registered), ever use of contraception, current use of contraception, persons (in addition to the spouse) who influenced the determination of family size (mother-in-law, relatives, neighbors, etc.), and number of wanted children. Families were classified into three categories according to their actual family planning: (1) full family planning--all the surviving births were a result of pre-planning, in which the spouses used contraception in order to control the number and timing of births; (2) partial family planning--only part of the surviving births were the result of pre-planning and controlling for the number and timing of children; and (3) no family planning--none of the births were the result of pre-planning or no attempt was made to practice contraception (or, if the spouses used some contraception, they were careless contraceptors or failed to use them properly). Actual family planning was accompanied by questions about preferred family planning. Answers were also categorized into three categories--full, partial, and none.

Our empirical examination of family planning and fertility includes, as an integral part, information on the independent variables of interest (socioeconomic modernization, westernization factors, and the status of the extended family and the hamula, etc.). Previous research has examined some macro aspects of fertility without detailed data on socioeconomic and political patterns. Linkages among those variables were made by inference rather than as part of an integrated analysis (for example, see Matras, 1973; Friedlander, Eisenbach, and Goldscheider, 1979).

Before approaching the data, we note that several studies have defined minority-majority status according to group size (see Johnson and Nishida, 1980). The definition used in our study is multidimensional (see chapter 2). In addition to group size, it includes economic dominance, political hegemony, external influence (as reflected in regional status and official and unofficial aid provided by external resources), and minority group feelings. Minority group status is viewed not as a constant but as a variable. Minority status may change over time in response to events (Frisbie and Bean, 1978). We emphasize the structural, rather than the psychological, factors associated with minority group status (see also Lopez and Sabagh, 1978; Ritchy, 1975).

It should be noted that minority-majority status is discussed at the community level. At the national level, all these groups are part of the Arab minority in Israel. Therefore, we do not ignore the fact that certain features (such as discrimination, hostility, etc.) that are the result of majority-minority relations at the national level do not necessarily exist at the communal level, or if they do, they do not always have the same effect and force. Nevertheless, previous study has shown that the status system deriving from minority majority relations is a valid basis for the analysis of social relations both at the communal level and at the societal level (see Al-Haj, 1985).

Contraception and Family Planning Services

In the community under research, modern methods of contraception are available for all. They are supported by the local family planning clinic and the medical center, "kupat holim". A minimal cost is required of any woman who wishes to have access to contraception. A nurse in the Infant Welfare Center ("tipat halav"--which offers free medical services for mothers and their children until five years of age) indicated that they make every effort to explain contraception to mothers and to encourage them to attend the clinic for family planning.

According to the interviews, almost all women have some idea about "inefficient methods" of contraception: rhythm, withdrawal, and other traditional methods. Eighty-five percent of the women reported that they have an idea about "efficient methods" (mainly the pill and IUD), the way to use them, and about the institutions offering family planning services. No considerable differences are observed among the various groups regarding the knowledge of efficient methods. The percentages are: 87 percent among Christians, 86 percent among local Moslems, 83 percent among in-migrant Moslems, 81 percent among local Druze, and 80 percent among Druze El-Jabal.

It appears that there were some differences among the several groups in practicing efficient methods during the 1950s and the 1960s. These differences have narrowed and have nearly disappeared at present. An in-depth interview with a physician, who had worked in Shefar-A'm since the late 1940s and was the only physician in the whole region during the 1950s, revealed that an official campaign to provide information about contraception for husbands and wives has been available in the locality since 1954.

It was very difficult at the beginning to interest spouses in our activity. Some even thought that we are foreign agents who aim to restrict their fertility. Others argued that we are working against the will of Allah-God, since "elli bijĩbu allah mnĩḥ"--everything given by God has to be accepted. Two years later, some spouses began to attend my clinic to receive information and even to practice contraception. All of them were Christians, almost no Moslems or Druze attended. The picture has changed since the early 1970s. Most of the married women--Christians, Moslems, and Druze--show a major interest in contraception and family planning services. Today about 80 percent of the married women receive information, this way or another, about family planning and the way they can control family size. But I want to indicate an interesting phenomenon. Almost nobody is interested in, or uses, contraceptives before the birth of the first, and sometimes the second, child. In some cases, three months after marriage women come, usually accompanied by the mother-in-law, to complain about the "delay" in their conception. I make every effort to convince them that during the first year after marriage the spouses have to enjoy their life without worrying about children. But unfortunately, nobody wants to listen. This phenomenon is observed among Moslems, Christians, and

Druze, but it is prominent in particular among the strangers (in-migrants).

Women are usually the initiators of family planning. But most likely this occurs with the support of husbands. Official institutions are prohibited from letting women practice contraception without the approval of their husbands. Even private physicians followed this rule. Otherwise, they might expose themselves to troubles. A local physician noted:

> I cannot forget one day when I pushed the door and entered my clinic; he started to curse me and to intimidate me. The thing I gave to his wife will cost me my life. At the beginning, I did not realize what is happening, but later he explained that I gave his wife contraceptives without asking him and despite his reluctance. The husband was pacified only when I explained to him that his wife only came for consultation and not to use contraception. This phenomenon has disappeared today. In many cases we do not ask women for the approval of husbands. We take this as granted because this has become a common phenomenon. Some women even feel insulted when we ask them for the approval of husbands. Since they feel that they have full authority ("bumūno") at home and they can convince the husbands about everything that supposed to be for the family interest ("fi maṣlaht el-eileh".

Despite the fact that wives are more active than husbands in initiating family planning, sometimes a reverse phenomenon is observed. Husbands approve and wives reject the use of contraception. This can be traced mainly to the desire of wives to have more children, in particular male children. As noted in Chapter 5, male children are considered an important resource of women's power within the family. This phenomenon, which was deeply seated in the agrarian period, persists despite the economic and the sociocultural changes which have taken place (see also Granquist, 1935; Galal el-Din, 1977). However, unlike during the agrarian period, the phenomenon of divorcing childless wives or wives without male children is rare today. This is because of the reinforcements in women status as noted earlier.

The data obtained from the local family planning clinic also indicates no considerable differences among the religious groups. Since the clinic was opened in 1976, it has served 685 women who have attended and practiced family planning. A progressive increase in the number of these women can be observed. Only 20 women practiced family planning through the clinic in 1976. This number increased to 89 in 1977, 109 in 1978, 143 in 1979, 156 in 1980, and 168 in 1981. Among the women served were 274 Moslems (40 percent of the total), 267 Christians (39 percent), and 144 Druze (21 percent). These figures are similar to the relative percentage of each religious group in the total population of the town. The main difference among the religious groups is that Christian women practice family planning at an earlier stage in the life cycle relative to women in the other groups. The percentage of women who attended the family planning clinic after having one or two surviving births is: 33 percent among Christians, 28 percent among Druze, and 22 percent among Moslems. Most of the Moslem and Druze women practiced contraception (for a period of three years and over) after completing their desired number of children. The percentage of women who started to practice family planning only after having five or more surviving births is: 34 percent among Christians, 42 percent among Druze, and 51 percent among Moslems.[2]

In sum, our findings clearly indicate that differentials in fertility and family planning are determined by the demand side of fertility, rather than by the access to contraception and family planning services. To further examine these differentials, we turn to the other direction of explanation suggested in our analysis.

Socioeconomic Characteristics, Minority Status, and Westernization

Our analysis in the preceding chapters has shown conspicuous differences among and within the religious groups in terms of socioeconomic characteristics, minority status, and family structure. Therefore, different conclusions are expected from the characteristics, minority status and westernization hypotheses.

The ordering of the groups according to their socioeconomic status from high to low is: Christians, local Moslems, in-migrant Moslems, local Druze, and Druze El-Jabal. According to the

----

[2] The subdivision of the religious groups between locals and in-migrants was not available from the data of the family planning clinic.

characteristics hypothesis, similar group ordering in terms of fertility and family planning is expected (from low to high in fertility and from high to low in family planning). Moreover, similar fertility and family planning patterns is also expected among the various groups at the same socioeconomic level.

In terms of minority-majority status, the in-migrant groups (in-migrant Moslems and Druze El-Jabal) are clearly minority groups compared to the locals. According to the minority status hypothesis, they are expected to have higher rates of fertility and lower rates of family planning than the locals. The ordering of the local groups is more complex because of their changing positions in the community status structure. However, Christians are expected to have the lowest rates of fertility (and the highest rates of family planning) because they have been a majority group for a long time. Their status is expected to have an accumulated impact on their fertility patterns. Local Moslems and local Druze are expected to have convergent patterns of fertility and family planning because of the convergence in their group status. Moreover, we would expect that at the highest level of socioeconomic status, the fertility of the in-migrant groups would drop below the fertility of the locals. Fertility and family planning among in-migrant groups and locals are expected to diverge for the old generation and to converge for the young generation because of the relatively advanced integration of the young generation.

The group ordering from high to low in terms of family nucleation, as measured by independence from the kinship group and the extended family, is: Druze El-Jabal, in-migrant Moslems, Christians, local Moslems and local Druze. According to the westernization hypothesis, we would expect the Druze El-Jabal to have the lowest rates of fertility (and the highest rates of family planning) followed by the other groups according to the same order of family nucleation. Therefore, in-migrant groups are expected to have lower fertility patterns than the locals.

To explore the differentials, we must first decide whether to treat each religious group as a whole or to take into consideration the group's internal divisions. Research conducted on several Arab Middle Eastern societies has shown that this point is controversial. Many of these studies have distinguished simply Moslems and Christians (Yaukey, 1961; Hanna, 1963). Chamie (1977) pointed out that treating each religious group as a whole is misleading. The evidence derived from our comprehensive survey supports the latter argument. Controlling for duration of marriage for women (ten years), noticeable differences in family

TABLE 3.2

HAMULA ORIENTATION BY HAMULA SIZE, EDUCATION, MASS MEDIA, AND FAMILY PLANNING: SHEFAR-A'M, 1983

Independent Variables	Social Role		Political Role		Economic Role	
	Attitude[1]	Behavior[2]	Attitude[3]	Behavior[4]	Attitude[5]	Behavior[6]
Hamula Size						
Small (less than 100 Hamula members in the same locality)	6.1	22.0	5.1	8.1	3.5	7.5
Moderate (100-500)	7.3	43.0	9.6	47.0	6.0	10.0
Large (500+)	8.0	57.0	16.5	66.7	7.0	10.0
Education						
No education - primary	8.2	45.1	25.8	31.0	10.0	9.8
High school - higher education	1.5	46.5	4.2	34.0	0.0	8.1
Mass Media Exposure						
Low	13.9	43.0	22.2	37.5	7.8	8.5
Moderate	6.5	40.0	12.9	34.1	5.5	9.1
High	0.0	39.0	3.3	35.7	0.0	9.6
Degree of Preferred Family Planning						
None	10.5	40.0	19.6	31.5	7.0	8.0
Partial	7.1	42.3	12.3	34.1	3.9	9.5
Full	0.0	36.0	2.1	32.0	4.8	9.0
Total proportion	7.6	38.0	15.1	34.6	6.0	9.0

N = 120

[1] Social Role, Attitude: approved right to cousin marriage

[2] Social Role, Behavior: married within the hamula

[3] Political Role, Attitude: approved hamula loyalty

[4] Political Role, Behavior: supported hamula based lists

[5] Economic Role, Attitude: perceived hamula affiliation as important to the individual's socioeconomic status

[6] Economic Role, Behavior: received hamula economic aid

137

size emerged between local and in-migrant groups (see Table 6.1).

The percentages of large families (five children and over) among the several groups are: 48 percent among in-migrant Moslems compared to 43 percent among local Moslems, and 44 percent among Druze El-Jabal compared to 38 percent among local Druze. Christians had the lowest percentage with large families--24 percent. Table 6.1 indicates there is a consistent group ordering along the several categories of family size, with the main differences in the extreme categories (small and large families). The differences among the several groups at the ideal family size level are negligible. The vast majority of the respondents prefer moderate families (3-4 children), and only a small minority prefer large families. This preference for a moderate family appears to be common among the several segments of Israeli society, Arabs as well as Jews (see Friedlander and Goldscheider, 1984).

Differences in family size are reflected in family planning, in actual behavior more than in attitudes. Overall, the data show that most of the spouses are practicing either partial (61 percent) or full family planning (28 percent). As for family size, group differentials in actual family planning emerge particularly in the polar categories of none and full family planning (Table 6.1). The ordering of the groups from high to low in family planning (and from low to high in family size) is: Christians, local Druze, local Moslems, Druze El-Jabal, and in-migrant Moslems.

This ordering differs from that expected by the characteristics hypothesis and the westernization hypothesis. Excluding Christians, no group is placed in terms of either family size or family planning according to that predicted by socioeconomic characteristics. Most prominent is the gap between the observed group ordering in family size and family planning, and the predicted by family nucleation. The observed is almost the opposite of the expected. The ordering of the several groups is most likely to be predicted by the minority status hypotheses. However, there is some convergence in the expectations of the characteristics and the minority status hypothesis. The expectations of the westernization hypothesis are completely different than the others.

It is remarkable that at the normative level (attitudes), no considerable differences emerge among the several groups, except for in-migrant Moslems who have the smallest proportion approving family planning and a small family size. We note that similar evidence emerged in Yaukey's study of Lebanon. While religious differentials were observed in actual fertility behavior, there were but negligible differentials in attitudes (Yaukey, 1961).

The consistency between attitudes and behavior has been a controversial issue in social psychology as well as in fertility studies (see Kar and Talbot, 1980; Westoff and Ryder, 1977). Our findings suggest a glaring gap between attitudes and actual behavior. In part, we accept the view that several independent variables can influence family planning directly and not through attitudes (Kar, 1978), and we suggest that a change in attitudes is not a sufficient condition for parallel changes in actual behavior.

This gap is not necessarily indicative of irrational behavior (Caldwell, 1977). It is the outcome of several objective factors. For considerable segments of the population, the question about attitudes is asked after they have already produced a number of children and have experienced the cost of having children. Therefore, their current attitude does not necessarily indicate their attitude before having children. Moreover, the data derived from the questions we asked about the reasons underlying partial or no family planning revealed some involuntary and voluntary factors. The most important among them was the lack of social support as reflected in the disapproval of the spouse or other members of the reference group (friends, neighbors, relatives, or others). Social costs (insecurity) were also a major consideration. This point emerged mainly among the older generation of the in-migrant groups who perceived children as a source of social security. For them, restricting the number of children meant threatening their social security.

We examine the relationship between socioeconomic status and fertility, using education as the measure of socioeconomic status. Education has been viewed as a major factor in the decline of fertility in western societies, and as a major factor in the changes in fertility in less developed nations (see Caldwell, 1982; Berelson, 1976). Literacy and educational achievement are social characteristics which are less likely to change in the adult population, since they are largely fixed during the pre-adult phase of the life cycle (Goldstein, 1972). Most importantly, education has been employed as the only measure of socioeconomic status by most studies of fertility differentials between minority and majority groups (see Goldscheider and Uhlenberg, 1969; Ritchy, 1975; Johnson, 1979). Therefore, it is important to use the same measure for comparison.

Overall, as indicated by several studies (see Goldstein, 1972; Berelson, 1976; Chaudhury, 1983), our findings suggest an inverse relationship between education and fertility and a positive relationship between education and family planning (both in actual behavior and attitudes). The analysis of group differentials in family planning by each group's level of education (see Table 6.2) reveals interesting findings. While a gap exists between minority-majority groups at the low and the middle categories, differentials decrease and almost disappear at the highest level. This indicates that actual family planning differentials are confined to those of low and moderate socioeconomic status. This finding also verifies the minority status hypothesis and contradicts the characteristics hypothesis. However, it differs from the minority status hypothesis in the sense that at highest level of socioeconomic status, the fertility patterns of the minority groups converge, rather than drop below those of the majority (for a similar conclusion see Ritchy, 1975).

Does this fact mean that the more integrated segments among the minority groups are the first to undergo the demographic transition to the small planned family? In order to examine this point, intergenerational comparisons were made. The respondents were divided into three groups according to marriage periods: (1) Before 1958, (2) 1959-1968, and (3) 1969-1981. Two categories which indicated high fertility were chosen: large families (5 children and over) and no family planning. Because of the ambiguity of reporting family planning during the first period, only family size was employed.

The findings shown in Table 6.3 indicate remarkable intergenerational differences in family planning and family size. While noticeable group differentials emerge between spouses married in the first and the second periods, they decrease drastically among the young generation, married in the third period. Intergenerational differences are observed among all the groups. In particular, they are prominent among the in-migrant groups. They emerge also in the perceived value of children as reflected in the detailed interviews. Among the older generation, most of the parents see children as a "source of security", as "compensation for the lost land", as a "source of power", and as a "means of integration in the community". For the young generation, children are seen as "the parents' continuity," and the children's success is perceived as a substitute for the "parents' success" and as a "source of pride". We can exemplify these points briefly by some typical interviews. A Moslem refugee (68 years old) said enthusiastically:

When we fled from our village (during the 1948 war), I couldn't take any of my property. We left our village empty-handed. When we moved to the town we were

140

TABLE 6.2

ACTUAL FAMILY PLANNING AMONG RELIGIOUS, LOCAL, AND
MIGRATORY GROUPS BY EDUCATION, SHEFAR-A'M, 1982*

Education and Family Planning	Local Groups			In-migrant Moslems
	Christians	Druze	Moslems	Moslems
No Education-primary				
No family planning	5.5	7.0	15.3	23.0
Partial	76.5	79.0	74.0	77.0
Full family planning	18.0	14.0	10.7	0.0
Total	100.0	100.0	100.0	100.0
High School				
No family planning	0.0	0.0	4.0	18.0
Partial	62.0	68.0	65.0	61.0
Full family planning	38.0	32.0	31.0	21.0
Total	100.0	100.0	100.0	100.0
Post Secondary				
No family planning	0.0	0.0	0.0	8.0
Partial	63.0	66.0	67.0	61.0
Full family planning	37.0	34.0	33.0	31.0
Total	100.0	100.0	100.0	100.0

N = 110

Source: Detailed interviews.

*Druze El-Jabal were omitted because they are not represented in
 the high levels of education, neither in the sample nor in the
 entire population of Shefar-A'm.

TABLE 6.3

ACTUAL FAMILY PLANNING AND FAMILY SIZE AMONG RELIGIOUS,
LOCAL, AND IN-MIGRANT GROUPS BY PERIOD OF MARRIAGE,
SHEFAR-A'M, 1982

Period of Marriage Family Planning Family Size	Local Groups			In-migrant Groups	
	Christians	Druze	Moslems	Moslems	Druze El-Jabal
Before 1958					
No family planning	-	-	-	-	-
Families of 5 children and over	61.0	75.0	81.0	95.0	92.0
1959-1968					
No family planning	8.0	11.0	15.0	19.0	15.0
Families of 5 children and over	58.0	72.0	79.0	87.0	82.0
1969-1981					
No family planning	3.0	4.5	5.0	6.0	4.5
Families of 5 children and over	45.0	51.0	55.0	59.0	55.0
N = 120					

Source: Detailed interviews.

142

"unnamed" people; nobody recognized us. We were helpless and needy, while in our original village we were wealthy, well known, and many needed our help. Children were the only property which remained at hand. I felt that I had to safeguard them. I was afraid to lose them like other things. I felt in need for more and more children, because they were the only thing I have.

Another interviewee from the Druze El-Jabal (60 years) said:

When we settled in Shefar-A'm (in the late 1950s), we were anonymous. We thought at the beginning that we can integrate in the community especially with the expected help of our brethren, the local Druze. But unfortunately we were rejected, whether by the municipality which didn't want to offer us any services, or by the local Druze who recognized that we existed only before the municipal election in order to gain our votes. I felt strongly like a stranger. I felt secure only when I was returning home to my wife and children. They gave me the feeling that there is somebody to care for and they want me.

Although the young generation of the in-migrant groups are still considered in a transitional status and not fully adjusted in the community, they did not suffer from the adjustment to the new environment or from being uprooted and thrown out as a powerless minority into a new milieu as did the older generation. Nevertheless, they suffered from being children in large families with restricted resources. A young refugee (32 years old) with a partial elementary education said:

After having the third child, my wife and I decided to stop bearing children. We don't want them to suffer like us from being children in a poor family. I was the elder son of a family of seven brothers and sisters. My father was an unskilled worker. He couldn't sustain us. Since I was the elder son I had to leave school in order to work and to gain more income for the family. However, I didn't find permanent work and my father wanted to return me to school. But I couldn't compensate my loss and I left school permanently even before completing the elementary level. Now I believe more and more that the number of children is not so important. It is more important to give them the

143

opportunity to succeed in life and to achieve their aspirations.

A young interviewee from the Druze El-Jabal (33 years old) with a secondary education and three children said:

> In my childhood I felt the lack of many things. I couldn't enjoy my childhood like the other children because of the difficult economic situation of my family. My father did his best in order to enable me to finish my secondary education. But I felt all the time his difficulties. The expenditure on my studies was at the expense of other important things for the family members. I wish to give my children all I can. I never want them to have a childhood like mine.

We may emphasize some points regarding the perceived value of children. The findings do not seem to contradict the argument that, for the older generation, the economic value of children played an important role, and that "the wealth flow" was mainly from children to parents or from elder children to the whole family (see also Caldwell, 1977). But this is not the major value of children, even for the older generation. The in-migrants who married right after their settlement in the 1950s, or were already married but had few or no children and completed their family size in the town, were from the beginning wage laborers. They lost their lands and no one worked in agriculture or in any job based in the domestic labor force. Moreover, during the first decade after the establishment of Israel, the whole country suffered from unemployment as a result of the Jewish mass immigration to Israel. A strong competition emerged for all jobs. Under these circumstances, children had little actual or even potential economic value and little potential to add to the family wealth. But the level of fertility was high among in-migrants during the first and the second decades (the 1950 and 1960s). We may hypothesize that the social significance of children is no less important than the economic one, and under conditions of social insecurity and instability, it may become the central motive for bearing children.

The perceived value of children for the young generation is well exemplified by the "altruism hypothesis" of Willis. He argues that "Altruist parents regard the success of their sons and daughters as a substitute for their own success. Technological change leads them to reduce their own consumption in order to increase their investment in their own offspring, who will live in a more productive and prosperous environment than their parents themselves do" (Willis, 1982:231). We disagree with Caldwell's argument, which implies that "family planning innovators", those who wish to and do control their fertility, are "more likely to have been spoiled", that is, those whose parents gave them more emotion and wealth than they expected back, leads them to treat their own children in a similar manner (Caldwell, 1977). This type of analysis may in part explain fertility regulation among the middle and the upper classes, but it does not explain the transition in fertility regulation among the majority of families located in the proletarian class. Our findings suggest that childhood experience plays a decisive role in determining fertility regulation behavior not only among parents who enjoyed relative parental indulgence in their childhood but also among parents who suffered in that period. For them, the control of family size means more investment in their children in order to enable them to achieve in ways that they could not obtain themselves. Therefore, change in the opportunity structure plays a major role in the differential response of the generations.

The westernization or the family nucleation hypothesis was examined by two main independent variables. Frequency of contact with Jews was used as an indicator of the degree of westernization, and marriage outside the kinship group was used as an indicator of family nucleation (see Matras, 1973; Avitsour, 1978). Contact with the Jewish population, who represents the agent of westernization, is expected to increase the exposure to western norms and culture, and as a result to increase the desire and the preference for family planning at the normative level as well as in terms of actual behavior.

Overall, Table 6.4 indicates a strong relationship among all the groups between preferred family planning (the normative level) and the degree of westernization. However, almost no relationship is observed in actual behavior. Contact with the Jewish population has but negligible effects on actual family planning even among the Druze, who are the most exposed to the Jewish sector. These findings were actually unexpected because the several groups as a whole noted intensive contact with the Jewish population and wide exposure to mass media: 61 percent of the respondents reported intensive contact with Jews, 63 percent reported that they read Hebrew newspapers, and 72 percent listened to the radio or viewed television regularly. This is part of a general trend taking place among Arabs in Israel and is reflected, among other ways, in the perception that biculturalism

TABLE 6.4

ACTUAL AND PREFERRED FAMILY PLANNING AMONG RELIGIOUS, LOCAL,
AND IN-MIGRANT GROUPS BY DEGREE OF WESTERNIZATION,
SHEFAR-A'M, 1982

Contact with Jewish People Family Planning	Local Groups			In-migrant Groups		
	Christians	Druze	Moslems	Moslems	Druze El-Jabal	Total
Intensive contact with Jews Actual family planning						
None	7.1	8.5	8.0	12.0	8.5	10.7
Partial	52.0	66.0	71.0	74.5	70.5	64.3
Full Total	40.9	25.5	21.0	13.5	21.0	25.0
Total	100.0	100.0	100.0	100.0	100.0	100.0
Preferred family planning						
None	0.0	4.0	7.0	10.0	0.0	7.5
Partial	20.0	24.0	23.0	40.0	24.5	21.6
Full	80.0	72.0	70.0	50.0	75.5	70.9
Total	100.0	100.0	100.0	100.0	100.0	100.0
Rarely-no contact Actual family planning						
None	4.5	6.5	12.0	17.0	12.0	12.6
Partial	58.0	62.0	65.0	70.0	71.0	57.5
Full	37.5	31.5	23.0	13.0	17.0	29.9
Total	100.0	100.0	100.0	100.0	100.0	100.0
Preferred family planning						
None	6.0	25.0	31.5	21.0	9.0	22.7
Partial	33.1	20.0	20.5	41.0	51.0	31.6
Full	60.9	55.0	48.0	38.0	40.0	45.7
Total	100.0	100.0	100.0	100.0	100.0	100.0

N = 15

Source: Detailed interviews.

146

and bilingualism are fundamental aspects of socioeconomic mobility (Smooha, 1984). Our examination of the reference groups reported by the respondents for several types of behavior connected with family lifestyles and socioeconomic achievement may shed light on this pattern (see Chapter 5). The vast majority of the respondents indicated that the Jewish population was the reference group in terms of socioeconomic achievement. But for family lifestyles, the reference groups were entirely local.

We had the opportunity to examine this point further in terms of contraceptive practice through data obtained from a survey conducted at the Family Planning Clinic. The attendants of the clinic (685 women) were asked to classify (according to their importance) the sources affecting their decision to practice family planning (contact with Jews, mass media, formal sources, movies, friends, neighbors, and relatives). The findings revealed the same picture as noted above: 60 percent of the respondents listed friends and neighbors as most important, 15 percent listed relatives, an other 15 percent listed formal sources--nurses, physicians, and social workers, and only 10 percent listed external sources (mainly mass media and contact with Jews).

Relationship with the kinship group was found to have a negligible effect on family planning, at the level of actual behavior as well as at the normative level. Among the spouses married within the kinship group, the percentages practicing full, actual family planning were: 36 percent among Christians, 30 percent among local Druze, 26 percent among local Moslems, 16 percent among in-migrant Moslems, and 22 percent among Druze El-Jabal. Among the spouses married outside the kinship group, the percentages were: 38, 24, 22, 14, and 17, respectively. It is remarkable that among local Druze, characterized by the highest percentage of patrilineal marriage (50 percent), a positive relationship was observed between this type of marriage and family planning. However, this relationship was very weak statistically. Therefore, family structure in terms of traditional kinship ties seems to have little direct effect on family planning. Similar evidence has characterized other areas, where a rapid massive adoption of modern fertility regulation occurred along with continuity of the extended family structure and kinship ties (see Freedman, 1979; Freedman, Chang, and Sun, 1982).

In sum, our analysis has demonstrated that family planning and fertility patterns are not uniform among Arabs in Israel. Differentials are observed between and among the religious groups. Treating the fertility of Arabs or Moslems as a whole may be misleading. These differentials are not the outcome of differential access to family planning services or of different levels of westernization, but rather are the outcome of the group status as determined by the nature of the relationships among the several groups within the community, on the one hand, and between the community and the wider society, on the other.

The minority group hypothesis proved to be most effective for our analysis. This does not imply that there are no socioeconomic effects. Socioeconomic factors were included among others as an integral part of our expanded definition of minority status. This means that socioeconomic characteristics per se do not account for fertility and family planning differentials among the religious groups. Nevertheless, they constitute an important component of the minority status.

The relationship between the normative level and the actual behavior in terms of fertility and family planning proved consistent with our findings regarding other aspects of family lifestyles, shown in the preceding chapters. A gap is observed between actual fertility behavior and fertility and family planning norms. A change in the normative level is not a sufficient assurance for a parallel change in fertility regulation and the transition to a small family size. Therefore, the convergence of the different groups at the level of actual behavior lags behind the convergence which has taken place at the normative level.

7

Conclusion

Our study has focused on the family lifestyles in an Arab urban community in Israel. It has demonstrated the importance of intensive community-level studies for the investigation of family patterns. Our analysis has shown that interaction among familial units, on the one hand and between these units and the broader population and development processes, on the other, is dynamic. This suggests the importance of the linkage between micro familial processes and macro sociological factors. The nature of the interaction among the familial units, the relationships among family members, women's status at home and in the community, and the interaction among group status and the family have been of crucial importance in affecting reproductive behavior and the several aspects of decision making within the family. This, in turn, has had major repercussions on the economic, political, and demographic structure of the community. At the same time, the family structure and the several processes in the familial units have been strongly affected by the broader political, economic, and demographic changes which have occurred over time in the community and in the society at large. The research strategy used in our study has exemplified the effectiveness of the combination among quantitative data, derived from the several kinds of surveys, and qualitative data, derived from in-depth interviews, document analysis, participant observation, and semi-structured conversations.

The experience derived from our field study suggests that a sole research method fails to describe the full picture. Hence, an adequate research strategy has to combine simultaneously several methods. Each method yields different types of data and facilitates the effective examination of specific aspects of the problem (see also Poplin, 1971; Caldwell, Reddy, and Caldwell, 1982). The comprehensive survey has been an effective way of deriving data on the basic characteristics of the family and the community. But some of the statistics obtained would have remained ambiguous, and even meaningless, without the qualitative data obtained from the in-depth interviews, participant observation, and the semi-structured conversations. These methods together have provided a broad, in-depth picture of family patterns. In order to understand the social, economic, and political contexts in which these patterns operate, and the factors underlying the trends which have occurred over time, there has been a need for community-level data which cover the present situation as well as the social history of the community. This was obtained by intensive document analysis. It is difficult, and may even be useless, to ask which method is more appropriate, since the different methods are integrative, rather than contradictory. In this sense, one method sheds light on, and furnishes the basis for, the other.

The micro method (document analysis) was used initially for the exploration of the basic characteristics of the community under research. After achieving this purpose, the use of the macro method (comprehensive survey) became more appropriate. Both methods furnished the basis for designing the cross-sectional sample for the in-depth interviews. The assessment of the data derived from these methods directed our selection of the focused surveys: the marriage survey and the family planning survey. The methods of participant observation and conversation with informants were treated as supplementary methods which were combined thoroughly with the other methods. The participant observation and the conversations were aimed mainly at supporting in-depth data about several points regarding family patterns and the nature of the interaction among the different groups in the community. Unlike the other methods, they were not focused on a specific aspect of a problem, but rather incorporated different aspects. The application of the several methods suggests the effectiveness of an open-ended strategy. A general framework which is pre-designed should leave room for unplanned, appropriate methods that can be added during the data collection. A continuous assessment of the findings throughout the field study may provide a useful base for selection of the unplanned methods.

Our analysis suggests the need for understanding the social history of the community and the preceding lifestyles for a better understanding of the current situation. The sole concentration on current lifestyles, while treating the past by inference, may be distorting. Dealing with change and continuity in family patterns necessitates a consistent analysis of the past, with which the present is compared. The analysis has shown that current processes in family life are the outcome of a synthesis of processes that took place in the past with those taking place at present.

Our analysis sheds light on some of the basic assumptions of the modernization approach. We have shown that diversification in the social structure and the family life is not restricted to the modern industrial period, but may emerge as well in agrarian societies, usually defined as traditional. In this sense, the shift in the wake of modernization is not from uniformity to diversity but from one form of diversity to another.

During the agrarian period, there were several social classes in Shefar-A'm: the merchant and the large landowners, the modest landowners, the small landowners, and the landless. Each stratum was connected with a unique type of family structure. Despite the similarities, each type had particular characteristics. While the modest and the large landowners maintained extended families which were the result of familial interest (in particular economic interest), the small landowners and the landless maintained extended families which were the result of necessity and the lack of other alternatives. The diversity in family life styles in the agrarian period was reflected as well in the status of women. There was no one typical status for women but several types which differed according to the level of social status, family type, and the stage in the life cycle. The extended family of the upper stratum, which was concentrated mainly among Druze and Christians, enhanced the status of women. Among the extended families of the modest and the lower strata, in which Moslems were overrepresented, women had the lowest status. Significant differences were observed between the status of women at the early period after marriage and their status at the advanced stages in the life cycle, where their status was conspicuously reinforced.

Diversity among contemporary Israeli Arabs is continuous with the past and has not been created in the wake of modernization; it is not the outcome solely of economic and sociocultural changes which occurred after the establishment of Israel. Although the vast majority of households have become nuclear in structure, a typical family structure has not been created. Groups and subgroups differ in the centrality of the kinship structure, in modes of women's status, particularly at the community level, and in fertility patterns. Even the small proportion of extended families which were observed covers several types: the business extended family, the agricultural family, and the extended family of residence.

The assumption that traditional structures are diminished as a result of modernization, and that the breakthrough of modernization is achieved by the breakdown of the antecedent traditional structure, proved to be misleading. We have shown that the kinship structure has been re-organized in an effective way and has become well integrated in the modern system. The hamula has become the main political unit in the democratic system of the municipal elections. It has become as well the main unit in the marriage market, despite the conspicuous modernization changes which occurred after the establishment of the state of Israel.

Sociodemographic factors played a decisive role in the reorganization of kinship groups in the post-state period. These included a rapid increase in the kinship group size as a result of a high natural increase, the lack of out-migration of the local groups, the collective in-migration of the refugees, and the residential density and concentration of descent groups. All these factors have led to the emergence of the kinship group as a major, local, potential source for social and political activities. The kinship group has been well exploited by its members as a way of exercising power and using resources. Integration of the "traditional" groups in the "modern" system has been enhanced by two main factors. On the one hand, modernization processes have changed the base of the local political system from a quasi-closed system, based on class-structure and socioeconomic stratification, to an open-system based on group size and group consolidation. On the other hand, modern opportunities have not been accompanied by the opportunity to form modern organizations. Competitive national and other formal organizations in place of local descent groups have not been available. This is because of the total dependency of the Arabs in Israel on the dominant Jewish sector, and because of their lack of access to the opportunity structure. Moreover, the residential-geographic concentration of kinship groups and the reduction of the external field of eligibles have contributed to the emergence of these groups as the central unit in the marriage market.

We may conclude that the shift to a participant society as a result of structural modernization exposes the power system to new forms of competition. Groups which had hitherto been at the periphery began moving towards the center and participating in the struggle for political control. Under conditions of localization and the lack of modern formal organizations, demographic features of the descent groups become a major source for deriving power and determining the competition. However, these demographic features, accompanied by a lack of external alternatives for matchmaking, also reinforce the social role of the descent group. But this role does not necessarily exist in order to serve the political alliances.

Despite the reinforcement of the kinship structure, some considerable changes were observed and documented. They reflect the drastic changes in the normative base of the hamula and the nature of the relationships and interactions among hamula members. The significance of the hamula and other descent groups lies in their reorganization as social, rather than biological, groups. The base of the kinship group is not necessarily the result of cultural or ideological factors, but is primarily the outcome of pragmatic constraints and structural opportunities.

A similar pattern was observed in the extended family and women's status. While drastic changes occurred in the structural elements of the extended family, fewer changes were observed in the associative elements, reflected in mutual aid, identification, and commitment among family members. Conspicuous changes occurred in the status of women at home, but fewer changes were observed at the community level. Even at the same level, some changes occurred more rapidly than others. While major improvements have taken place in the educational attainments of women, the occupational attainments, and political and social activities of women still have lagged behind. Moreover, a reverse trend was noticed in the productivity of women. The drastic economic changes which took place after the establishment of Israel resulted, among other things, in a drastic decrease in the economic role of women and a decline in their participation in the labor force.

We may conclude that modernization occurs through complex processes of diversification, rather than through uniform overall processes. Extended family units, which may be defined as traditional, may continue to exist along with changes in the nature of the relationships among family members. Therefore, the definition of extended family relations or kinship ties as traditional is distorting. The modernization approach, which leaves no room for so-called traditional groups and structures, does not encompass the diverse features of the developing process taking place in developing societies.

Our analysis points to the importance of distinguishing among attitudes and norms on the one hand, and actual behavior, on the other. Treating family attitudes and family behavior as synonymous is misleading. In this sense, the assumption of the modernization approach that psychological modernity is a sufficient condition for actual modernization is incorrect. The analysis of the several familial units during the different periods has shown that a glaring gap exists between the normative-ideological level and the actual behavior. Normative changes may precede or lag behind changes in actual behavior. While a conspicuous change has been observed in the normative base of the kinship structure and the extended family, this has not been the case for actual behavior.

Similar patterns emerged from our analysis of fertility regulations. While convergence in fertility has occurred among the several groups at the normative level, considerable differences are still observed in terms of family size and family planning practices. In the case of women's status, changes in the normative level have lagged behind changes in actual behavior. While fewer changes have been observed in the ideological-normative system, which emphasizes the inferiority of women and their subordination to men, conspicuous changes have occurred in women's status at home and, in some aspects, at the community level.

We may conclude that processes of modernization are determined more by structural than cultural or psychological factors. The move from a traditional to a modern level of family life depends mainly on the combination of the availability of structural modernizing factors and the availability of alternative patterns of actual behavior. These are determined to a large extent by the nature and the magnitude of access to the opportunity structure. In this sense, the convergence in level of modernization among the developed center and the developing periphery is not necessarily a question of time, since modernization changes may reinforce, rather than diminish, dependence and inequality. We have shown that the Arab minority in Israel has become more and more dependent on the Jewish dominant sector. Paradoxically, the Jewish sector, which has introduced some important modernization patterns for Arabs in Israel, has restricted at the same time their access to some major modern institutions as a result of the increasing dependence process. Therefore, to some extent, the modernization of Arabs has remained partial (for discussion of partial modernization, see Rueschemeyer, 1976). It does not appear that this trend will be changed in the near future unless conspicuous structural changes

154

take place, which would give Arabs more access to the opportunity structure and more alternatives for change.

However, such convergence in the modernization level among Jews and Arabs does not imply a total adoption by the Arabs of the dominant Jewish values. We have demonstrated that individuals and groups have several reference groups, at the same time and at various levels. The reference group for socioeconomic attainment among Arabs is the external Jewish sector, the dependency center, which has control over the opportunity structure. The reference groups for fertility, family planning, and other family lifestyles are primary groups like families and other local groups where daily, intensive and informal social interaction takes place. In addition, the contact with the Jewish population, who constitute the agents of westernization, is perceived by some segments of the community as having a negative effect on women's status. This is due to the fear that this contact may expose women to different cultures, which contradict major values of the modesty of women and the family's honor.

The analysis of the group status structure in Shefar-A'm using the framework of minority-majority relations suggested that this model, which is usually applied to the analysis of the societal level, is also a valid basis for the analysis of the community level. In this sense, a given society is not divided only among a majority and a minority, but the minority itself may include several groups which have a minority or majority status. Our research suggests the importance of adopting a multidimensional definition of minority status. In addition to group size, minority status includes actual and psychological elements. Moreover, minority status has to be viewed as dynamic rather than stable. It may change over time in response to events.

Our analysis of the status structure in Shefar-A'm throughout the several periods revealed that the status elements operate in a differential manner. During the Mandatory Period, though Moslems were the regional majority, they were a minority with respect to the factors of economic dominance and political control. The Druze were a majority from the viewpoint of economic dominance, but in all other aspects were a minority. The Christians were a minority with respect to their regional position, but were a majority with respect to other elements of social status.

Our examination of minority status feelings also shows that the type of subjective status feelings are not dichotomous but continuous. A given group can find itself not at the extremes but somewhere between majority and minority feelings. This was the

155

pattern for the Christian community during the pre-State period when it did not have unambiguous majority feelings because of its status as a regional minority which from time to time was subject to outside threats. These ambivalent feelings continued to exist after the establishment of the State of Israel. The Druze, on the other hand, moved from strong minority feelings during the Mandatory Period to a sense of strength after Israeli independance. The feelings of the Moslem community also passed through various stages. Before 1948, Moslems had a sense of strength because they were a regional majority. Later, following the 1948 war, their sense of weakness and crisis was sharp, while in the 1960s, they experienced a swift transition to majority feelings as a result of and changes in the internal status system.

A comparison of the objective and the subjective elements of status feelings shows that there is no necessary positive correlation among them. A given group can have a minority status in accordance with objective factors, and nevertheless have subjective majority feelings. On the other hand, a group can also have most of the important factors of a majority status and, at the same time, have strong minority feelings.

Minority status is determined mainly by structural, rather than psychological, elements. Therefore, status replacement in the community and minority integration within the majority are affected by structural factors and by the nature of the social interaction among the several groups. This was reflected in the status replacement among Moslems and Christians in the late 1960s and the status of the second generation of the in-migrant groups. The new status of Moslems and of the second generation of the in-migrant group may be defined as transitional. In this sense, it is useful to take into consideration the existence of a transitional status among minority and majority categories.

The status structure has deeply affected family lifestyles. The local power system has been determined by the interaction between family structure and religious group. During the pre-State period, the interaction took place between the extended family and the religious group. In the post-1948 period, interaction shifted to between the kinship structure and religious group. Also all the lists in the local elections are based on hamulas from the same religious group. There appears to be two levels of competition over the local power system: the first is among family groups over the representation of the religious group, and the second is among the religious groups over the control of the local power system.

The group status structure also affected the patterns of

fertility of the several groups. The long-term majority status of the Christians has had a cumulative effect on their fertility, which has always been the lowest compared to the other groups. Changes in the status structure that occurred after the establishment of Israel were reflected in the patterns of fertility and fertility regulations. A convergence in fertility and family planning was found among the several groups at the highest status. Moreover, the transitional status of Moslems and second generation in-migrants is reflected in their fertility transition towards a small family size. Those with a transitional status perceive the reduction of family size as a means of further assimilation, by stressing the quality rather than the quantity of children. This trend is reinforced by their tendency to prevent their children from experiencing the difficult childhood they had, of growing up in large families with restricted resources.

Throughout our analysis we have shown that family lifestyles are the outcome of the interaction taking place at five main levels: the individual, familial, group, communal, and societal levels. Each level may affect family patterns directly or indirectly through interaction with other levels. The effect among levels may be mutual, not necessarily one-way. However, this mutuality does not imply symmetry. It appears that the influence of the broader on the smaller level is greater than that in the other direction. Therefore, the several levels may affect family patterns in a diverse, rather than a uniform, manner. The extent of the effect of each level on family life may differ within the same family at different points in the life cycle, among groups and subgroups at the same time, and over time in response to changes in the broader political, economic, and sociocultural contexts. Hence, a longitudinal analysis of the dynamic of the interaction among the family and the differential levels is of crucial importance. Clearly, an examination of family patterns which fails to take into consideration the effect of the several levels, currently and over time, is incomplete.

Unlike the modernization approach, our analysis suggests that activity of individuals is not restricted to the modern phase but may be observed as well in agrarian traditional societies. The assumption that in traditional societies the individual is submerged within the family and other collective networks proved to be misleading. Evidence derived from the elections in the Ottoman period (1915) revealed the importance of individual bases. Moreover, even the extended family, in which most of the family members take a small role in the family decision making, has been always headed by an individual, the patriarch father, who controlled the family property and strongly influenced family affairs. At advanced stages of the life cycle, after the fragmentation of the extended family, each of the sons created his own family and became residentially and economically independent. This constituted the basis for the creation of a new extended household. The sons who were dependent at earlier stages of the life cycle later became heads of households and the center of dependency for the other family members. Our analysis has demonstrated that women, who have always been viewed as powerless in the extended family, exerted a great pressure on husbands which resulted in the earlier fragmentation of the extended family. The transition from the status of daughter-in-law to mother-in-law with the marriage of the sons granted women a greater amount of influence on the family members and on family affairs.

The modernization process increased, rather than created, the importance of individuals at the family and the community levels. The shift to a participant society after the establishment of Israel increased the individual's social and political activity and his potential to affect the family affairs. The modernization changes which occurred in the community have resulted, among other things, in earlier fragmentation of the extended family and the creation of independent nuclear households at earlier stages of the life cycle. We may conclude that one of the main differences among traditional and modern societies may lie in the timing at which an individual's activity and independence are observed. In modern society, the activity of individuals at the family and the community levels begins at a relatively earlier stage in the life cycle than in traditional society.

Our analysis has shown that the interaction and the effects among the several familial units are not uniform. The relationships and the commitments are much stronger between the nuclear and the extended family than between the familial units and the kinship group. While the affiliation with the extended family is mostly biological, since it bears commitments as well as rights of inheritance, the affiliation with the kinship groups can be social as well as biological. We have demonstrated that a person can be affiliated with a certain hamula by a fictive relationship. Moreover, the internal refugees have created a new form of kinship group based on affiliation to the original community, rather than to the great grandfather, in order to meet their social and political needs. Therefore, studies which have overemphasized the strong role of the hamula in affecting fertility patterns and other aspects of decision making within the nuclear family have to be reconsidered (see Caldwell, 1977; Pat Caldwell, 1977; Matras, 1977; Patai, 1967). The role of the hamula lies mainly at the communal level, rather than at the level of affecting the internal affairs of the basic familial units.

As anticipated, the group affects family patterns through the social class and the group status structure. We may add that unlike the assumption of the modernization approach, modernization factors have not necessarily resulted in weakening religious or ethnic groups. On the contrary, modernization may reinforce these groups. Our analysis has shown that the shift to a participant society in which the power system is determined by group size and the ability to form tight networks has reinforced the cohesion of the hamula as well as the religious group.

The extent of the independent effect of the communal level on the group and the family levels differs according to the extent of the economic and political independence of the community. We have shown that the nature of the relationships among the several social units within the community has completely changed since the establishment of Israel. This is mainly because of the shift in the groups as a whole from inter-communal dependence to dependence on the dominant Jewish sector. Therefore, individual, family, and group socioeconomic attainments are determined at the societal level, rather than at the communal level. In the pre-1948 period, the relationships of the population of Shefar-A'm with the surrounding communities in the region had considerable repercussions on the group and the family life. This was because of the economic dependence which existed among Shefar-A'm and these communities. The shift to overall dependency of the Arab communities, including Shefar-A'm, on the external center drastically decreased social relations among Arab communities, and has, in turn, affected family patterns. This has been reflected in the decrease in extra-local marriages and the disappearance of effect of the regional aid on the group status structure in the community.

The direction of dependency between the communal and the societal levels determines the direction of effect between the two levels. Asymmetric relations between them create a parallel asymmetry in the direction of effects. In this sense, the effect of the majority status at the local level on the minority status at the societal level is derived from the local community and can not serve as a basis for changing the minority status of Arabs within Israeli society. The local groups remain either as a minority within the minority or as a majority within the minority. Hence, a consideration of the effects of minority group status needs to take into account the status at both the community and the societal levels.

While our analysis is based on one community, it does not appear to be unique or idiosyncratic. Comparisons made throughout our analysis with other studies suggest that this case study exemplifies general processes taking place among Arabs in Israel and, with reservations, can be generalized more broadly to Middle Eastern societies as well as developing societies in the Third World defined as transitional. It is clear that the particular conditions in Shefar-A'm are unique and the constellation of factors are specific to Arab communities in Israel. Nevertheless, the processes underlying family lifestyles may characterize other people and cultures. Our research has pointed to a clear need for more intensive community-level studies encompassing simultaneously the several familial units into one integrative research. The community-level variables and the social history of the community have to be viewed as an integral part of the explanatory variables. Methodologically, there is a need for adopting a research strategy which includes a mixture of macro and micro methods (see also Caldwell, Reddy, and Caldwell, 1982). In this sense, social research may benefit from the use of an interdisciplinary approach. An effective combination of sociological, anthropological and demographic approaches may enhance our in-depth understanding of social phenomena and the several aspects of population and development. Our study suggests more intensive research is needed on pluralistic communities adopting a dynamic multi-dimensional approach of minority-majority status to further explore the role of ethnic, religious, and other descent groups in social structure and social change. Our study will be valuable if it contributes to the recommended research directions. The multi-level approach employed in this study will, hopefully, enrich studies emphasizing the complexity and the diversity in family patterns and development processes in developing societies.

Bibliography

Abrammovitz, Z., and I. Guelfat. 1944. *The Arab Economy in Palestine and Middle Eastern Countries* (Hebrew). Tel-Aviv: Hakibbutz Hameuchad.

Abu-Gosh, Subhi. 1972. "The Election Campaign in the Arab Sector." In *The Elections in Israel 1969*. Ed. Alan Arian. Jerusalem: Jerusalem Academic Press, pp. 239-252.

Alfaruqi, Lois Ibsen. 1978. "An Extended Family Model from Islamic Culture." *Journal of Comparative Family Studies* 9(2):243-255.

Al-Haj, Majid. 1985. "Ethnic Relations in an Arab Town in Israel." In *Studies in Israeli Ethnicity: After the Ingathering*. Ed. Alex Weingrod. New York: Gordon and Breach Science Publishers.

_____. 1979. *The Status of the Arab Hamula in Israel*. Unpublished Masters Thesis. University of Haifa: Department of Sociology and Anthropology (Hebrew).

Al-Qazzaz, A. 1975. "Women in the Arab World: An Annotated Bibliography." Detroit: Association of Arab-American University Graduate.

Allman, James. 1978. "Family Patterns, Women's Status and Fertility in Middle East and North Africa." *International*

Journal of Sociology of the Family 18(2):19-34.

Al-Nouri, Qais. 1980. "Changing Marriage Patterns in Libya: Attitudes of University Students." *Journal of Comparative Family Studies* 11(2) (Spring):219-255.

Antoun, Richard. 1972. *Arab Village: A Social Structural Study of Trans-Jordanian Peasant Community.* Bloomington: Indiana University.

_____. 1968. "On the Modesty of Women in an Arab Muslim Village: A Study in Accommodation of Tradition." *American Anthropologist* 70:671-697.

Aries, Philippe. 1971. "From the Medieval to Modern Family." In *Family in Transition.* Eds. A. Skolnick and J. Skolnick. Boston:Little Brown and Company, pp. 91-104.

Armer, Michael, and Robert Youtz. 1971. "Formal Education and Individual Modernity in an African Society." *American Journal of Sociology* 76(4):604-626.

Arnon, Isaac, and Michael Raviv. 1980. *From Fellah to Farmer.* Rehovot: Settlement Study Center.

Avitsour, Mordechai. 1978. "The Village Taibeh: Transformation and Process of Change." *Hevra Verevaha* 1(1) (March):22-33 (Hebrew).

Barakat, Halim. 1973. "The Palestinian Refugees: An Uprooted Community Seeking Repatriation." *International Migration Review* 7 (Summer):147-161.

Baruch, Nissim. 1966. *The Development of the City Nazareth and the Means Towards Economic Advancement* (Hebrew). (Mimeographed). Tel-Aviv: Yiuts Vemihkar.

Ben-Amram, Eliyahu. 1965. "A Demographic Description of the Arab Population in Israel" (Hebrew). *Hamizrah Hehadash* 15(1-2):7-24.

Ben-Shahar, Haim, and Emanuel Marx. 1972. *Arab Cooperation, A Socio-economic Study.* Part A-B (Hebrew) (Mimeographed). Tel-Aviv: Israel Institute for Research

162

and Information.

Berelson, B. 1976. "Social Science Research on Population." *Population and Development Review* 2(2) (June):219-266.

Berger, Monroe. 1962. *The Arab World Today.* New York:Doubleday and Company, Inc.

Bilsborrow, Richard E. 1981. *Surveys of Internal Migration in Low-Income Countries: The Need for and Content of Community-Level Variables.* Working Paper No. 104, Geneva: International Labor Office, pp. 1-63.

Blau, Peter. 1960. "Structural Effects." *American Sociological Review* 25(2):178-193.

Blood, Robert O. Jr., and Donald M. Wolfe. 1960. *Husbands and Wives: The Dynamic of Married Living.* New York: The Free Press.

Boserup, Ester. 1970. *Women's Role in Economic Development.* New York: St. Martin's Press.

Bossen, Laurel. 1975. "Women in Modernizing Societies." *American Ethnologist* 3 (November):587-601.

Caldwell, John C. 1982. *Theory of Fertility Decline.* London: Academic Press.

_____. 1977. "Towards a Restatement of Demographic Transition Theory." In *The Persistence of High Fertility.* Ed. John C. Caldwell. Canberra: Australian National University. Also in *Population and Development Review* 2, 3, 4 (September and December):321-366 (1976).

_____, P.H. Reddy and P. Caldwell. 1982. "The Micro Approach in Demographic Investigation: Toward a Methodology." Social Science Research Council and Population Council, Proceedings of a Conference on Innovative Approaches to Research on Demographic and Socioeconomic Change in Latin America through the Study of Family and Household. August.

Caldwell, Pat. 1977. "Egypt and the Arabic and the Islamic Worlds." In *The Persistence of High Fertility*. Ed. John Caldwell. Canberra: Australian National University, pp. 593-616.

Canaan, A. 1931. "Unwritten Laws Affecting the Arab Women of Palestine." *Journal of Palestine Oriental Society* 11:172-203.

Chamie, Joseph. 1977. "Religious Differentials in Fertility: Lebanon, 1971." *Population Studies* 31(2):365-382.

Chaudhury, Raphiqul Huda. 1983. "The Influence of Female Education, Labor Force Participation and Age at Marriage on Fertility Behavior in Bangladesh." Brown University:Population Studies and Training Center Working Papers WP-83-06.

Chevallier, Dominique. 1971. *LaSociete Du Mon Liban*. A Lepdque Dela Revolution Industrielle En Europe. Paris: Labrairie Orientaliste Paul Geuthner.

Cohen, Abner. 1965. *Arab Border Villages in Israel*. Manchester: Manchester University Press.

Cromwell, Ronald, and David H. Olson, (eds.). 1975. *Power in Families*. New York: Halsted Press.

Datan (Dowty), Nancy. 1972. "To Be a Woman in Israel." *The School Review* 80(2) (February):319-332.

Davis, James, Joe L. Speath and Carolyn Houson. 1961. "A Technique for Analyzing the Effects of Group Composition." *American Sociological Review* 26(2):215-225.

Dixon, Ruth. 1971. "Explaining Cross-Cultural Variation in Age at Marriage and Proportions Never Marrying." *Population Studies* 25 (July):215-230.

DosSantos, Theotonio. 1984. "The Structure of Dependence." In *The Gap Between Rich and Poor*. Ed. Mitchell A. Seligson. Boulder: Westview Press, pp. 95-104.

Eisenbach, Zvi. 1978. *Trends and Changes in Fertility of the Moslem Population of Israel.* Doctoral Dissertation. Jerusalem: Hebrew University (Hebrew).

Eisenstadt, S.N. 1975. "The Influence of Traditional and Colonial Political System on Development of Post-traditional Social and Political Orders." In *Modernization in South-East Asia.* Ed. Hans-Dieter Evers. London: Oxford University Press.

El-Anba. 1983. August 7. "The Druze of Shefar-A'm Discuss the Situation of their Brethren in Lebanon."

Elliot, Joyce, and William Moskoff. 1983. "Decision-Making Power in Romanian Families." *Journal of Comparative Family Studies* 14(1) (Spring):39-50.

Evers, Hans-Dieter, ed. 1975. *Modernization in South-East Asia.* London: Oxford University Press.

Falah, Salman. 1974. *The History of the Druze in Israel* (Hebrew). Jerusalem: Prime Minister's Office.

Farid, Samir. 1984. *World Fertility Survey: Fertility Patterns in the Arab Region.* London: World Fertility Survey, 1972-1984 Symposium.

Fernea, Robert and James Malarkey. 1975. "Anthropology of the Middle East and North Africa: A Critical Assessment." *Annual Review of Anthropology* 4:183-206.

Findley, Sally. 1982. "Methods of Linking Community-Level Variables with Migration Survey Data." In United Nations ESCAP, *National Migration Surveys: X Guidelines for Analysis.* New York: United Nations, pp. 276-311.

Ford, Thomas and Gordon DeJong, eds. 1970. *Social Demography.* Englewood Cliffs: Prentice-Hall, Inc.

Fox, G.L. 1973. "Another Look at the Comparative Resource Model: Assessing the Balance of Power in Turkish Families." *Journal of Marriage and the Family* 35 (November):718-730.

Freedman, Ronald. 1979. "Theories of Fertility Decline: A

Reappraisal." *Social Forces* 58 (September):1-17.

_____, Ming-Cheng Chang and Te-Hsiung Sun. 1982. "Household Composition, Extended Kinship and Reproduction in Taiwan: 1973-1980." *Population Studies* 36(3) (November):395-411.

Freundlich E., and N. Hino. 1984. "Consanguineous Marriage Among Rural Arabs in Israel." *The Journal of Medical Sciences* 20:1035-1038.

Friedlander, Dov, and Calvin Goldscheider. 1984. "Israel's Population: The Challenge of Pluralism." *Population Bulletin* 39(2) (April):3-38.

_____. 1979. *The Population of Israel.* New York: Columbia University Press.

Friedlander, Dov, Zvi Eisenbach and Calvin Goldscheider. 1979. "Modernization Patterns and Fertility Change: The Arab Population of Israel and the Israel Administered Territories." *Population Studies* 33(2):239-254.

Frisbie, Park, and Frank Bean. 1978. "Some Issues in the Demographic Study of Racial and Ethnic Population." In *The Demography of Racial and Ethnic Groups.* Ed. Frank Bean and Parker Frisbie. New York: Academic Press.

Galal el Din, Mohamed ElAwad. 1977. "The Rationality of High Fertility in Urban Sudan." In *The Persistence of High Fertility.* Ed. John Caldwell. Canberra: Australian National University, pp. 633-658.

Ginat, Joseph. 1981. *Employment as a Factor of Social Change in the Arab Village.* (Mimeographed). Tel-Aviv: Sapir Center and Shiloah Center, Tel-Aviv University (Hebrew). ·

_____. 1975. *A Rural Arab Community in Israel: Marriage Patterns and Women's Status.* Doctoral Dissertation. Salt Lake City, Utah: University of Utah.

Golani, Gideon, and Avraham Katz. 1963. "Urban Geography of Shefar-A'm City" (Hebrew). *Teva Vearetz* 6(7-8):309-315.

Goldscheider, Calvin. 1983. "The Adjustment of Migrants in Large Cities of Less Developed Countries: Some Comparative Observations." In *Urban Migrants in Developing Nations*. Ed. Calvin Goldscheider. Boulder, CO: Westview Press, pp. 233-253.

_____. 1981. "Societal Change and Demographic Transitions." Chaire Quetelet, Belgium, *Population and Social Structure:* 83-106.

_____ and Peter R. Uhlenberg. 1969. "Minority Group Status and Fertility." *American Journal of Sociology* 74(4):361-72.

Goldstein, Sidney. 1972. "The Influence of Labour Force Participation and Education on Fertility in Thailand." *Population Studies* 26(3):419-436.

Goode, William J. 1982. *The Family* (Second Edition). New Jersey: Prentice-Hall.

_____. 1963. *World Revolution and Family Patterns*. New York: Free Press.

Gore, M.S. 1965. "The Traditional Indian Family." In *Comparative Family Systems*. Ed. M.F. Nimkoff. Boston: Houghton Mifflin Company, pp. 209-232.

Government of Palestine. 1947. *General Monthly Bulletin of Current Statistics* Vol. 7, No. 2, Department of Statistics.

Granquist, Hilma. 1935. *Marriage Conditions in a Palestinian Village*. I and II. Commentationes Humanarum. Helsingfors: Societas Scientrarium Fennica.

Gulick, John. 1968. "Culture Change and Psychological Adjustment in Arab Society and the Middle East." Paper presented at the 8th Congress of Anthropological and Ethnological Sciences, Tokyo-Kyoto, September 3-10.

Gusfield, Joseph. 1967. "Tradition and Modernity: Misplaced Polarities in the Study of Social Change." *American Journal of Sociology* 72:351-362.

167

Habash, Awni. 1977. *Processes of Change and Modernization in the Arab Family: A Survey in an Arab Village in Israel* (Mimeographed). Jerusalem: The Institute for Labor and Welfare: Hebrew University (Hebrew).

Haines, David, Dorothy Rutherford and Patrick Thomas. 1981. "Family and Community Among Vietnamese Refugees." *International Migration Review* 15(1):310-319.

Hanna, Rizik. 1963. "Social and Psychological Factors Affecting Fertility in the United Arab Republic." *Marriage and Family Living* 25:69-73.

Hechter, M. 1975. *Internal Colonialism: The Celtic Fringe in British National Development, 1536-1960.* University of California Press.

Hillery, George A., Jr. 1955. "Definition of Community: Areas of Agreement." *Rural Sociology* 20 (June):118.

Horowitz, D., and R. Hinden. 1938. *Economic Survey of Palestine.* Tel-Aviv: Economic Research Institute of the Jewish Agency for Palestine.

Hugo, Graeme. 1981. "Village-Community Ties, Village Norms, and Ethnic and Social Networks: A Review of Evidence from the Third World." In *Migration Decision Making.* Eds. Gordon F. DeJong and Robert W. Gardner. New York: Pergamon Press, pp. 186-224.

Inkeles, Alex, and David Smith. 1974. *Becoming Modern: Individual Change in Six Developing Countries.* Cambridge: Harvard University Press.

Israel, The Central Bureau of Statistics. 1983. *Statistical Abstract of Israel.* No. 34.

_____. The Minorities Ministry. 1949. *Report on the Minorities Ministry Activities.* (Mimeographed) May, 1948 - January, 1949 (Hebrew).

Israely, Amihoud. 1976. "The Employment Revolution Among Non-Jewish Minorities of Israel." *Hamizrah Hehadash* 26(3-4):232-239 (Hebrew).

The Jerusalem Post, January 10, 1984. "Shamir Meets Bedouin Leaders."

Johnson, Nan. 1979. "Minority Group Status and the Fertility of Black Americans, 1970: A New Look." *American Journal of Sociology* 84(6):1386-1400.

Johnson, Nan, and Ryoko Nishida. 1980. "Minority Group Status and Fertility: A Study of Japanese and Chinese in Hawaii and California." *American Journal of Sociology* 86(3):496-511.

Kanaana, Sharif. 1975. "Modernization and the Extended Family: The Arab Minority in Israel." *The Wisconsin Sociologist* 12(1) (Winter):3-19.

_____. 1975a. "Toward the Refinement of Individual Modernity Scales." *Indian Journal of Comparative Sociology* 2(1) (August):20-29.

Kar, Snehendu. 1978. "Consistency between Fertility Attitudes and Behavior: A Conceptual Model." *Population Studies* 32(1):173-185.

_____ and John M. Talbot. 1980. "Attitudinal and Nonattitudinal Determinants of Contraception: A Cross-Cultural Study." *Studies in Family Planning* 11(2) (February):51-64.

Katz, Ruth and Yochanan Peres. 1985. "Is Resource Theory Equally Applicable to Wives and Husbands?" *Journal of Comparative Family Studies* 16(1) (Spring):1-10.

Khuri, Fuad. 1976. "A Profile of Family Association in Two Suburbs of Beirut." In *Mediterranean Family Structure*. Ed. J.G. Perstiany. London: Cambridge University Press, pp. 81-100.

Kressel, Gideon. 1976. *Individuality Against Tribality: The Dynamic of a Bedouin Community in the Process of Urbanization (Hebrew)*. Tel-Aviv: Hakibutz Hameuchad.

Landau, Jacob M. 1972. "The Arab Vote." In *The Elections in-*

Israel 1969. Ed. Alan Arian. Jerusalem: Jerusalem Academic Press, pp. 253-263.

Layish, Aharon. 1977. "Compensation to Divorced Women in the Druze Family." *Israel Law Review* 12(3) (July)330-343.

_____. 1975. "Social and Political Change in Arab Society in Israel." In *The Palestians*. Eds. Michael Curtis, Joseph Neyer, Chaim Waxman and Alleh Pollach. New Brunswick, N.J.: Transaction Books.

Lee, Gray, and Larry Petersen. 1983. "Conjugal Power and Spousal Resources in Patriarchal Cultures." *Journal of Comparative Family Studies* 14(1) (Spring):23-38.

Lerner, Daniel. 1964. *The Passing of Traditional Society. Modernizing the Middle East.* London:The Free Press of Glencoe.

Levy, Marion J. Jr. 1965. "Aspects of the Analysis of Family Structure." In *Aspects of the Analysis of Family Structure.* Ed. Ansley Coale. Princeton: Princeton University Press.

Linenberg, Ron. 1971. "The Penetration of National Parties into the Druze Village Daliat Elkarmel" (Hebrew). *Medinah Vemimshal* 1(1):125-144.

Lopez, David E., and Georges Sabagh. 1978. "Untangling Structural and Normative Aspects of the Minority Status - Fertility Hypothesis." *American Journal of Sociology* 83 (6):1491-1497.

Lustick, Ian. 1980. *Arabs in the Jewish State: Israel's Control of a National Minority.* Austin, Texas: University of Texas Press.

Lutfiyya, Abdulla. 1970. "The Family." In *Reading in Arab Middle Eastern Societies and Cultures.* Eds. Abdulla Lutfiyya and Charles Churchill. The Hague: Mouton, pp. 505-525.

Maoz, Moshe. 1962. "Local Government in Arab Settlements in Israel" (Hebrew). *Hamizrah Hehadash* 12(3-4):233-240.

Mari, Sami. 1978. *Arab Education in Israel.* Syracuse, N.Y.: Syracuse University Press.

Matras, Judah. 1973. "On the Changing Matchmaking, Marriage and Fertility in Israel: Some Findings, Problems and Hypothesis." *American Journal of Sociology* 79(2) (September):364-388.

McNicoll, Geoffrey. 1983. "The Nature of Institutional and Community Effects on Demographic Behavior: An Overview." Working Paper. Center for Policy Studies.

Merton, Robert. 1968. *Social Theory and Social Structure.* (Enlarged Edition). New York: The Free Press.

Miro, Carmen, and Joseph Potter. 1980. "Social Science and Development Policy: The Potential Impact of Population Research." *Population and Development Review* 6(3) (September):421-440.

Murty, Krishna Radha, and Susan Devos. 1984. "Ethnic Differences in Contraceptive Use in Sri Lanka." *Studies in Family Planning* 15(5):222-232.

Nakhleh, Khalil. 1975. "The Direction of Local-level Conflict in Two Arab Villages in Israel." *American Ethnologist* 23 (August):497-516.

Nettle, J.P., and R. Robertson. 1968. *International System and Modernization of Societies: The Formation of National Goals and Attitudes.* New York: Basic.

Nimkoff, M.F., and R. Middleton. 1960. "Types of Family and Types of Economy." *The American Journal of Sociology* 3:215-225.

Palmore, James, Robert Klein and Affin bin Marzuki. 1970. "Class and Family in a Modern Society." *American Journal of Sociology* 76(3):375-397.

Patai, Raphael. 1983. *The Arab Mind.* Revised Edition. New York: Charles Scribner's Sons.

_____. 1970. "Cousin Right in Middle Eastern

Marriage." In *Readings in Arab Middle Eastern Societies and Cultures.* Ed. A. Lutfiyya and C. Churchill. The Hague: Mouton, pp. 535-559.

_____. 1967. *Golden River to Golden Road.* Philadelphia: University of Pennsylvania Press.

Pelzel, John. 1970. "Japanese Kinship: A Comparison." In *Family and Kinship in Chinese Society.* Ed. Maurice Freedman. Stanford: Stanford University Press, pp. 227-248.

Peretz, Don. 1958. *Israel and the Palestine Arabs.* Washington, D.C.: The Middle East Institute.

Poplin, Dennis. 1972. *Communities. A Survey of Theories and Methods of Research.* New York: The MacMillan Company.

Portes, Alejandro. 1976. "On the Sociology of National Development: Theories and Issues." *American Journal of Sociology* 82 (July):55-85.

Ritchey, P. Neal. 1975. "The Effect of Minority Group Status on Fertility: A Re-examination of Concepts." *Population Studies* 29 (July):249-57.

Rodman, H. 1972. "Marital Power and the Theory of Resources in Cultural Context." *Journal of Comparative Family Studies* 3:50-69.

Rogers, Susan Carol. 1975. "Female Forms of Power and the Myth of Male Dominance: A Model of Female/Male Interaction in Peasant Society." *American Ethnologist* 2 (November):727-756.

Rosenfeld, Henry. 1980. "Men and Women in Arab Peasant to Proletariat Transformation." In *Theory and Practice.* Ed. Stanley Diamond. The Hague: Mouton, pp. 195-219.

_____. 1973. "Hamula." *Journal of Peasant Studies* 1:243-244.

_____. 1972. "Patrilineal Endogamy in the Arab

Village in Israel" (Hebrew). *Rivon Lemehkar Hevrati* 1:41-62.

_____. 1972a. "An Overview and Critique of the Literature." In *Rural Politics and Social Change in the Middle East*. Eds. Richard Antoun and Iliya Harik. Bloomington: Indiana University Press, pp. 45-74.

_____. 1968. "Change, Barriers to Change and Contradictions in the Arab Village Family." *American Anthropologist* 70,(4):732-752.

_____. 1964. "From Peasantry to Wage Labour and Residual Peasantry: The Transformation of an Arab Village," in *Proccess and Pattern in Culture*. Ed. Robert A. Manners. Chicago: Aldin, pp. 211-234.

_____. 1962. "The Arab Village Proletariat" . *New Outlook* 5(3) (March-April):7-16.

_____. 1960. "On Determinants of the Status of Arab Village Women." *Man* 60:66-70.

_____. 1958. "Processes of Structural Change Within the Arab Village Extended Family." *American Anthropologist* 60(6):1127-1139.

Rueschemeyer, Dietrich. 1976. "Partial Modernization." In *Explorations in General Theory in Social Science. Essays in Honor of Talcott Parsons*. Eds. Joue Louber, Raines C. Baum, Andrews Effrat and Victor M. Lidz. New York: Free Press, Vol. II, pp. 756-772.

Sabri, Muhsin. 1973. "The Legal Status of Israeli Arabs" (Hebrew). *Iyone Mishpat 3(2) (September):568-581*.

Sayigh, Rosemary. 1979. *Palestinians: From Peasants to Revolutionaries*. London:Zed Press.

Schneider, David. 1965. "Kinship and Biology." In *Aspects of the Analysis of Family Structure*. Ed. Ansley J. Coale. Princeton: Princeton Press, pp. 83-101.

Segev, Tom. 1984. *The First Israelis-1949*. Jerusalem: The

Domino Press (Hebrew).

Seligson, Mitchell. 1984. "Inequality in a Global Perspective: Directions for Further Research." In *The Gap Between Rich and Poor.* Ed. Mitchell A. Seligson. Boulder: Westview Press, pp. 397-408.

Shils, Edward. 1965. *Political Development in the New States.* Englewood Cliffs: Prentice Hall.

Shnaiberg, Alan. 1970. "Measuring Modernism: Theoretical and Empirical Exploration." *American Journal of Sociology* 76(3):399-425.

Shokeid, Moshe. 1980. "Ethnic Identity and the Position of Women among Arabs in an Israeli Town." *Ethnic and Racial Studies* 3(2):188-206.

Smooha, Sammy. 1984. *The Orientation and the Politicization of the Arab Minority in Israel.* Haifa: The Jewish Arab Center. Monograph Series on the Middle East No. 2.

_____. 1984a. *Social Research on Arabs in Israel, 1977-1982: A Bibliography.* University of Haifa: The Jewish-Arab Center, Institute of Middle Eastern Studies.

_____. 1980. "Control of Minorities in Israel and Northern Ireland." *Comparative Studies in Society and History* 22(2):256-280.

_____. 1978. *Israel: Pluralism and Conflict.* London: Routledge and Kegan Paul.

_____. 1976. "Arabs and Jews in Israel: Minority-Majority Relations" (Hebrew). *Megamot* 22(4) (September):397-423.

Smooha, Sammy, and Ora Cibulski. 1978. *Social Research on Arabs in Israel, 1948-1977.* Ramat Gan: Turtledove Publishing.

Soffer, Aron. 1981. "Populating Israel's Mountains While Preserving their Environmental Quality." *Environmental Conservation* 8(2) (Summer):151-158.

Spengler, Joseph. 1974. *Population Change, Modernization and Welfare*. Englewood Cliffs: Prentice-Hall.

Stein, Kenneth. 1984. *The Land Question in Palestine, 1917-1939*. Chapel Hill: The University of North Carolina Press.

Stendel, Ori. 1973. *The Minorities in Israel: Trends in the Development of Arab and Druze Communities 1948-1973*. Jerusalem: The Israel Economist.

Tamari, Salim. 1981. "Building Other People's Homes: The Palestinian Peasant's Household and Work in Israel." *Journal of Palestine Studies:* 31-63.

Tel-Aviv University. 1979. *Agriculture in the Arab Sector* (Mimeographed). Tel-Aviv: The Shiloah Center for Middle Eastern and African Studies (Hebrew).

Tippes, Dean. 1973. " Modernization Theory and Comparative Study of Societies: A Critical Perspective." *Comparative Study in Society and History* 15:199-225.

Valenzuela, Samuel and Arturo Valenzuela. 1984. "Modernization and Dependency: Alternative Perspectives in the Study of Latin American Underdevelopment." In *The Gap Between Rich and Poor*. Ed. Mitchell Seligson. Boulder: Westview Press, pp. 105-118.

Van Dusen, Roxann. 1976. "The Study of Women in the Middle East: Some Thoughts." *Middle East Studies Association Bulletin* 10(2):1-9.

Warren, Ronald. 1956. "Toward a Reformulation of Community Theory." *Human Organization* 15 (Summer):8.

Waschitz, Joseph. 1947. *The Arabs in Palestine*. Tel-Aviv: Siphriat Poalim (Hebrew).

Wertheim, W.F. 1975. "Resistence to Change From Whom?." In *Modernization in South-East Asia*. Ed. Hans-Dieter Evers. London: Oxford University Press.

Westoff, Charles and Norman Ryder. 1977. "The Predictive Validity of Reproductive Intentions." *Demography* 14(4) (November):431-453.

Willis, Robert. 1982. "The Direction of Intergenerational Transfers and Demographic Transition: The Caldwell Hypothesis Re-examined." In *Income Distribution and Family*. Ed. Y. Ben-Porath. *Population and Development Review:* A Supplement to Vol. 8, 1982:207-234.

Wrigley, E.A. 1969. *Population and History*. New York: McGraw-Hill Book Company.

Wrong, Dennis. 1977. *Population and Society*. (Fourth Edition). New York: Random House, Inc.

Yaukey, David. 1961. *Fertility Differences in a Modernizing Country: A Survey of Lebanese Couples*. Princeton: Princeton University Press.

Zahalka. Salman. 1976. "Manpower in the Arab Sector" (Hebrew). *Rivon Lekalkala* 23(9) (August):195-209.